The Big Book of Questions & Answers about Jesus

Sinclair B. Ferguson

CF4·K

FOR JONATHAN
AND OTHERS LIKE HIM

© Copyright 2000 Sinclair B. Ferguson
Published by Christian Focus Publications Ltd
Geanies House, Fearn, Tain, Ross-shire,
IV20 1TW, Scotland, U.K.
www.christianfocus.com

Published in 2000
Reprinted 2001, 2005 and 2008

Illustrations by Diane Matthes
Cover preparation by Douglas McConnach

ISBN 978-1-85792-559-3

Scripture quotations are from *The New International Version*
1973, 1978, 1984 by the International Bible Society.

Printed by W S Bookwell, Finland

CONTENTS

PAGES

FOR PARENTS OR LEADERS

In order to help you get the most out of this material we have supplemented the text by giving suggestions for activities. These aim to help the child understand the ideas being presented.

Write down / compile information / keep a diary

Think about the issues being talked about, possibly leading to action being taken.

Draw a poster / make something / be creative. A special notebook and a supply of paper for posters will help here.

Take some action! Possibly providing support through prayer or practical help.

Find out information from the Bible or other relevant reading material.

Short passages from the Bible for further reading are suggested.

A short prayer is given to bring the activities to a close.

Short questions encourage thought and discussion of the questions and answers.

All ages can enjoy learning.

You will be amazed as you go through this book with a child how much you discover yourself. Some congregations and study groups have based their adult teaching programme on the topics and subjects raised in *The Big Book of Questions and Answers*. Learning together like this helps families to continue their learning through prayer and family discussion times during the week. It is an excellent way for children and adults to learn about God together.

Do you have lots of questions about Jesus?

* Sometimes teachers can tell us the answers

* Sometimes others can help us

* Sometimes we find out the answer ourselves by reading a book

But we have many questions about Jesus that only Jesus himself can answer.

Perhaps you never ask these questions out loud. But you ask them inside. You think about them when you are on your own.
Sometimes you lie awake in bed thinking about them.
Where can you find the answers?

Jesus answers our questions about himself in the Bible. Most of them are answered in the four books we call The Gospels.

Gospel is a word that means 'good news'.

The Big Book of Questions and Answers about Jesus will help you to find out more about Jesus.
I have written it for you!
I hope you enjoy using it as much as I have enjoyed writing it!

Sinclair B Ferguson

WHEN JESUS WAS A BOY

Questions
1 to 5

1. WHAT DOES THE NAME JESUS MEAN?

Dads and mums usually choose a name for their baby *before* the baby is born.

Sometimes they choose two names: one if you turn out to be a boy, and another if you're a girl!

So you probably got your name before anybody knew very much about you!

It's good to have a name, isn't it? You wouldn't much like being just a number, would you?

Babies' names are usually chosen for a reason. There are all kinds of reasons. Maybe the parents just liked the name.

Some mums and dads chose their baby's name because someone else in the family had it. Sometimes it's because of somebody well-known they hope their baby will be like.

God chose Jesus' name for him.

He chose it for him before anybody else knew exactly when he was coming into the world.

Most names have a meaning. Sometimes names come from other languages. In those languages the word means something special.

Did you know that the name Jesus is really the same as the name Joshua? It comes from two Hebrew words which mean *the Lord saves*.

God sent an angel called Gabriel to tell Mary that she was going to have a baby boy. Gabriel means *Man of God*. Mary means *bitter*.

Mary was probably only about sixteen at the time. She loved God very much and wanted to serve him. Gabriel told Mary that when the baby was born she was to call him Jesus.

Mary was going to marry a man called Joseph. He was a very good man. God sent his angel to Joseph as well to let him know about Jesus. The angel told Joseph what was going to happen. He explained why this name was so important.

Gabriel said to Joseph: 'Jesus will save his people from their sins'.

So, right from the start of his life, Mary and Joseph knew what Jesus was going to do.

They must have thought a lot about what the angel said.

They must have wondered: How is Jesus going to do this?

That is one of the things we are going to try to discover in *The Big Book of Questions and Answers about Jesus*.

Each bit of *The Big Book* will tell you something more about Jesus.

1

Question

What does the name Jesus mean?

Answer

The name Jesus means: 'The Lord saves'.

One day in Old Testament times, God spoke to Moses from inside a burning bush! Moses asked God: 'Who are you? Do you have a name I can call you?'
God said: 'I am who I am. Call me 'I AM'.'

So from then on God's people called him I AM. In Hebrew his name was Yahweh. Yahweh said to Moses: 'I have come to save the people from their slavery in Egypt and to take them into a new land. I will save them.'

The man who led them into the promised land was called Yahweh Saves. His name was Joshua. But God knew we would need another kind of salvation from another kind of slavery. He promised he would send a Saviour.

For years and years God's plan was hidden from almost everybody. But God told bits of his plan to men called prophets. They learned that a Saviour would come. They wrote down what God told them so that the secret wouldn't be lost. So when Jesus was born, some people were waiting for the Saviour. They weren't sure who the Saviour was. But they knew he would come. Jesus is that Saviour. That is why he was called: The Lord Saves.

Memory Verse

You are to give him the name Jesus, because he will save his people from their sins.

Matthew chapter 1, verse 21.

ACTIVITIES

Read Matthew chapter 1, verses 18-25 to discover how Jesus got his name.

TALKING TIME:

Ask your mum or dad if your name means anything special. Why were you given your name? Do you have brothers and sisters? What do their names mean?

ACTION TIME:

Turn up Exodus chapter 3 in the Bible. Draw a picture of what is described there – with God's words coming out of the bush.

PRAYER TIME:

Lord Jesus, I am so glad that you have a name I can use when I speak to you. Thank you for being so willing to come into this world to be our Saviour. Help me to trust you to be my Saviour.
Amen.

2. WHERE AND WHEN DID JESUS LIVE?

Jesus was born in Bethlehem in the land of Judea.
The Romans ruled the world then. They had a kind of king, who was called Caesar. He allowed other countries to have their own kings—so long as they did what he wanted them to do. So they weren't real kings at all. In Judea the name of the king was Herod. He was not a good man.

One of these Roman kings, called Caesar Augustus had decided to have what is called a census. In a census all kinds of information about people is written down. It helps the government to decide what to do. Some countries today have a census every ten years.

Caesar Augustus wanted to raise taxes. He wanted money to help him rule the Roman Empire. He needed to build roads; he needed to pay his soldiers. Lots of money was needed.

Nowadays in a census, every family just gets a form to fill in.
In those days, everyone had to go to the original home town of their family.

Joseph and Mary lived in Nazareth. They had to go to Bethlehem.
That was a journey of about 90 miles.

Jesus was just about to be born. The journey must have been a very hard one for Mary.

When they got to Bethlehem, it was full of people. There was no room for them anywhere. But an innkeeper allowed them to use his stable. Isn't that amazing? Jesus was born in a stable for animals.

People came to visit the baby Jesus. Shepherds and strange wise men from the East came to see him. Someone else wanted to come to see Jesus. That someone else was King Herod.

When King Herod heard about the birth of a new king, he wanted to get rid of him. To make sure, he planned to kill all the baby boys born in Bethlehem under two years old.

Joseph took Mary and Jesus as far away as possible – they ended up in Egypt. Then, when Herod died, they all moved back home to Nazareth. Jesus grew up in Nazareth. Later on he seems to have moved to Capernaum which is near the Sea of Galilee.

All this happened two thousand years ago.

2

Question
Where and when did Jesus live?

Answer
Jesus was born about two thousand years ago in Bethlehem, and then went to live in Nazareth, where he grew up.

Jesus is a real person. He had experiences like ours. Some of them must have been very difficult.

He was not born in a nice hospital, but probably in a cave.
When he was a little boy he had to be taken to another country because the King was trying to kill him.
He lived in this world in the little town of Nazareth. He watched Joseph making things out of wood; he went to school; he had to do his homework.
Jesus began life as a very small baby; he grew up to be a boy. Then he became a teenager. Finally he became a full grown man.

For a long time Jesus just lived quietly, loving his Heavenly Father. He experienced the same kinds of things you do.
That is how we know he understands what it is like for us.

Memory Verse
She wrapped him in cloths and placed him in a manger, because there was no room for them in the inn.
                    Luke chapter 2, verse 7.

ACTIVITIES

READING TIME

Read Matthew chapter 2, verses 1-23 to find out what adventures Jesus had when he was still a little boy.

TALKING TIME:
Ask your mum what it was like to look after you in the first few years of your life. Ask your dad what he thinks it must have been like for Joseph to look after Mary and Jesus when they were in Egypt.

ACTION TIME:

Look up a map of Palestine at the back of a Bible. Draw an outline of it and then fill in the places where Jesus lived at different times.

PRAYER TIME:
Lord Jesus, I didn't really know much about the danger you were in when you came into this world.
You are so good and loving and I find it hard to understand why Herod was so angry and wanted to get rid of you.
I know that not everyone loves you. But help me to love you. I know others may treat me badly because I follow you. Help me to remember all that you suffered for me, and to be brave for you.
Amen.

3. WHAT WAS SPECIAL ABOUT JESUS?

Jesus had some unusual things happen to him even when he was a baby. Remember how he had to be taken away into Egypt because King Herod was trying to kill him?

Eventually, when Joseph and Mary arrived back in Nazareth they lived in an ordinary home. Jesus was brought up the same way other little boys were.

But there were some things about him that made him different and very special.

We know what one of them was: his name described what he was to do. He was to be our Saviour.

But there was something else.

In the Old Testament, God had given promises about the person he would send to be the Saviour. The men who told the people about these promises were called prophets.

One of these prophets, whose name was Isaiah, told the people that God would send a special baby.
This baby would come into the world in a special way.

We all come into the world through a father and a mother. But this baby would not come that way. God would show that he was special and different. He would bring him into the world through a mother alone.
When Jesus began his life inside his mum, the Bible says she wasn't married yet to Joseph.
Joseph was Jesus' guardian, not his father!

But what was so special about Jesus?
Isaiah explained by telling the people that he would be called *Immanuel*. That means 'God with us'.
Jesus was a real human, like us.
But he was also different; he was God.
That was why he had to come into the world in a new way.
He was God and man!

He was special in one other way.
Jesus never sinned.

3

Question
What was special about Jesus?

Answer
Jesus was God as well as man.

Usually people teach us about things we don't understand by saying 'It is like this.'
Since Jesus alone is God and man, we can't really say 'It's easy to understand; it's like this.'
We can't really understand how Jesus can be both God and man. But the Gospels show us that he was.
He did the kinds of things God does.
Jesus rules over nature – he stilled a storm.
Jesus can make people better – he healed the sick.
Jesus could even bring dead people back to life.
Jesus could do what only God can do: he could forgive sins.

Yet Jesus was a real man. Jesus felt pain. Jesus got tired. He cried. And Jesus died.

Because he is a real man he understands us.
Because he is God he has power to help us.

Memory Verse
The virgin shall be with child and will give birth to a son, and they will call him Immanuel – which means, 'God with us'.
Matthew chapter 1, verse 23.

ACTIVITIES

READING TIME

Read Luke chapter 1, verses 29-38 to discover how Jesus was Mary's son, and yet God's Son.

TALKING TIME:
Can you imagine some of the things that Jesus experienced when he was growing up that would show he was really human?

ACTION TIME:
Draw five faces:

A happy face
A puzzled face
A serious face
An angry face
A sad face with tears

Would Jesus have had all of these faces, or just some of them?

PRAYER TIME:
Lord Jesus, I can't really understand how you can be God as well as man. But I want to thank you that because you became a baby and then a boy and then a man you can understand me. And I am so glad that you are God. You have the power and strength to help me.

I love you very much. Please help me to know you and to love you even more.
Amen.

4. WHAT WAS JESUS LIKE WHEN HE WAS YOUNG?

Jesus had a pretty hair-raising time as a baby. Can you imagine being bundled up and taken by your mum and dad to a country miles away, where they speak a different language? Well, that's what happened to Jesus. Herod the King was trying to get rid of him. Actually, this wasn't the last time people tried to kill Jesus. But eventually King Herod died, and Joseph and Mary were able to go back to Nazareth.

Joseph was a carpenter. He made things out of wood. He probably made all kinds of things like chairs and tables. But he would also have made things like plates and bowls out of wood. He would have made doors and windows for houses, and sometimes even whole roofs! Then he would have made tools and carts for other workmen, and ploughs and yokes for the farmers. A carpenter was a very important person to have around.

Joseph taught Jesus to be a carpenter too. When he was young, Jesus probably had his own little set of tools to use. Maybe Joseph made them for him. Perhaps he had kept the ones his dad had made for him when he was small.

Not long before Jesus was born there was a new law in his land which meant that all the boys had to go to school until they were teenagers (girls were taught at home by their mums!). What would Jesus have thought about that? Jesus learned to read and write and count. Most important of all, we know that Jesus learned to read and to memorize the Bible. He learned big, long passages off by heart.

When Jesus was twelve, Joseph and Mary took him to visit the Temple in Jerusalem for one of the feasts. They went in a big crowd with their friends and relatives. Everybody looked after everybody else. It was very safe, and so nobody worried about where the children were.

When they were coming home, Mary and Joseph suddenly realised that they hadn't seen Jesus for ages! Nobody knew where he was. So they went back to Jerusalem to look for him.

At last they found him. He was in the Temple. He was asking the teachers questions about the Bible. The teachers were amazed. Jesus seemed to ask really important questions—and sometimes he gave answers to the questions himself—answers that the teachers hadn't thought of!

Sometimes mums get a bit upset. Mary was very upset that day! 'Mum' said Jesus, calming her down, 'You should have known I would be in my Father's house!'. Mary and Joseph were really puzzled.

Mary watched Jesus very carefully after that. He got bigger. He seemed to get wiser and wiser. People loved him. God loved him. What Mary noticed most of all was how kind and loving and obedient he was to Joseph and herself.

4

Question

What was Jesus like when he was young?

Answer

Jesus went to school, worked with his hands, loved his family and loved God as his Heavenly Father.

Some grown ups think that we can't understand things about God when we're young.
That wasn't true of Jesus—and it isn't true of us.

Like Jesus, we can learn God's Word, the Bible.
Like Jesus, we can ask questions about God and his love.
Sometimes we can see things in the Bible older people don't see!

Jesus thought about what God says so much that he always seemed to know exactly what God wanted him to do.

But Jesus did more than that: he obeyed God's Word.
He kept God's commandment: 'Honour—love and obey—your father and mother.'
Jesus honoured Mary and Joseph. Although he had come from heaven, he wanted to do what they said.
Jesus loved God. He also loved Mary and Joseph, even when they didn't really understand him.

Memory Verse

Jesus grew in wisdom and stature, and in favour with God and men.
> Luke chapter 2, verse 52.

ACTIVITIES

READING TIME

Read Luke chapter 2, verses 41 to 51.

This is the only passage in the whole Bible that tells us what Jesus did when he was a boy.

TALKING TIME:

How can you be more like Jesus? What does mum think? What does dad think? If you have any brothers and sisters, can you imagine what they think? What do you think?

ACTION TIME:

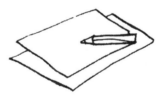

Imagine you were in Jesus' house for a week when he was young.
Make a chart for each morning, afternoon and evening of the week. Fill in what you think Jesus would be doing. (Remember that there was a day of rest or a Sabbath Day on Saturday!)

PRAYER TIME:

Lord Jesus, it is marvellous that at one time you were exactly my age! You know what it is like to have to learn things at home and school.
Please be with me, so that I can follow your wonderful example. Help me to love and obey my dad and mum.
Amen.

5. HOW DID JESUS KNOW WHAT GOD WANTED HIM TO DO?

Jesus had some adventures as a boy. He was taken away to Egypt. He was lost by Mary and Joseph. They must have wondered: What is going to happen next?

Both Joseph and Mary had been told by God that Jesus was special. But they didn't really understand what God wanted him to do. Don't you think they must have talked about that together when Jesus was asleep?

How could Jesus find out what God wanted him to do?

Jesus was learning to study the Bible. He didn't have a copy of it himself, but he was learning it at school. He tried to remember it, and so he knew whole chapters off by heart. He could think about its meaning while he was working with his tools. He thought about it when he went for walks. He spent time in prayer, talking to his Father.

In the Scroll of Isaiah there was a passage Jesus loved. It described someone who would be God's perfect servant. This passage even told Jesus what God's servant said. Jesus realised it was really talking about him. He was to be God's servant!
Here is the passage:

> Morning by morning God wakes me up;
> He whispers in my ear so that I can hear everything he says.
> He has helped me to understand what he is saying,
> And I have been obedient.
> I have never turned away from what he has told me.

There were other passages in the Bible that Jesus saw were speaking about him.

Some of these passages were also in the Scroll of Isaiah. They spoke more about this person called The Servant of the Lord. These passages said that the Servant would suffer and die for the sins of others.

There was another passage, this time in the Scroll of Daniel, which described a Son of Man who would become God's king. Then there were other passages which spoke about the Son of God.

No one knew who these three people were.

But Jesus realised that these three people weren't three different people.
The Suffering Servant and the Son of Man and the Son of God were one and the same person.

That person was Jesus himself!

5

Question

How did Jesus know what God wanted him to do?

Answer

Jesus learned God's will for his life by reading, thinking about, and obeying God's word, the Bible.

When Jesus began to think about the Bible, he must have seen that God had given a promise right at the beginning: he would send a Saviour.
That promise can be found in Genesis 3 verse 15. It says that someone would come who would be a Great Conqueror and Deliverer.

Slowly, down through the centuries, God added more hints to help people understand better who this Saviour would be.
He told the people about a king who would come. He explained that they would need a much greater priest than any priest they had ever had. He promised he would send them a prophet who would explain everything to them.

But only Jesus held the key to understand who this person was.
Jesus himself is the key.
The whole Bible pointed to him.
He is the Saviour God promised.

Memory Verse

The Sovereign Lord . . .wakens me morning by morning, wakens my ear to listen like one being taught.
        Isaiah chapter 50, verse 4.

ACTIVITIES

READING TIME

Read Luke chapter 4, verses 11 to 21 to discover one time when Jesus told people:'These verses speak about me.'

TALKING TIME:

Can you and your family think of a plan that would help you to get to know God's Word, the Bible, better?

ACTION TIME:

Get ready to read through The Gospel according to Mark. This is a big task! Get out a Bible that has headings for the different stories in it.

Make a chart for the next two months. Write in the passage you will read, or get mum or dad to read to you each day.
Then, when you have finished The Big Book, start reading through The Gospel of Mark each day.

PRAYER TIME:

Lord Jesus, you read and thought about the Bible. You understood it. Please help me to read it too, and to understand it. Then, help me to see what you want me to do each day. Thank you for your love for me. Thank you for the help you give to me. Amen.

WHEN JESUS LEFT HOME

Questions
6 and 7

6 WHY WAS JESUS BAPTISED?

Jesus' Bible was what we call the Old Testament. As he thought about what his Bible said, he saw God's plan for his life. Jesus knew that the time would come for him to leave his family home.

So, when Jesus was about thirty years old he left home. He began to preach and to do wonderful things.
But before that, there was something he needed to do.

Jesus had a relative called John. John was just a few months older than Jesus.

Like Jesus, John had been thinking about the promises God had given. God had shown him that the Promised Saviour, the King God was going to send, would definitely come – and he would come soon.
John knew that the people were not ready for God's king. So he started to preach.
John's message was this: 'The king is coming soon. You had better be ready.' He told them to turn away from their sins and get ready. As a sign of this, he baptised them in the River Jordan. It was a sign of their sins being washed away.
Thousands came to listen to John. He told them that God's king was going to come very soon. They promised to turn away from their sins. John baptised them.

One day when John was baptising, he saw that Jesus was in the crowd waiting to be baptised. Jesus didn't need to be baptised for himself. John said 'Jesus, you should be baptising me!'

But Jesus had come to be our Saviour.
He knew that he would have to take the great burden of our sins and become a sacrifice to God for them. So he said to John: 'Baptise me, John. One day I am going to take the place of all these sinful people who are confessing their sins.'

So John baptised Jesus.

Something dove shaped came down on Jesus. John knew this was a sign of God's Spirit coming on Jesus. He knew then that it was Jesus who was God's king.

Jesus heard God speaking to him. God said, 'Jesus, you are my Son. I love you. Your obedience makes me very happy.'

So Jesus was baptised surrounded by sinners. It was a sign that he would be their Saviour.

Jesus knew what nobody else knew. One day he would die on the cross. He would be surrounded by sinners then as well.

6

Question
Why was Jesus baptised?

Answer
Jesus was baptised as a sign that he had come to take away the sins of the world.

In the Old Testament God gave the people lots of signs. They were pictures of his love for them. Some of these signs showed the people what they needed most from God.
One sign God gave was the sign of washing with water. It was a sign of how we need to be made clean from our sins. God's people washed even pots and pans as a sign that God wanted them to be clean in everything they did.

John the Baptist used water as a sign. When he baptised people it was a sign of how God can wash away the sin in our hearts. Jesus had no sins of his own that needed to be washed away. He came to take away our sins. Our sins had to be placed on Jesus.

When Jesus was baptised it was as if he was going into water made dirty by the sins of the people who had gone into it to be baptised. It was as if their dirty sins were poured over him. Jesus knew that was what would really happen on the cross.

Memory Verse
John saw Jesus coming towards him and said: 'Look, the Lamb of God, who takes away the sin of the world.'
John chapter 1, verse 29.

ACTIVITIES

READING TIME

Read John chapter 1, verses 19-34 to find out all that happened when Jesus was baptised.

TALKING TIME:
Have you been baptised? What do you think baptism is a sign of today?

ACTION TIME:
Can you draw a picture of someone being baptised? Underneath it, complete this sentence:

Baptism means . .

PRAYER TIME:
Lord Jesus, thank you for coming to be my Saviour. Thank you so much for being baptised in the River Jordan as a sign that you would take my sins. And thank you for going all the way from there to the Cross and dying for me. I love you and want you to be my Friend.
Amen.

7. WHAT HAPPENED TO JESUS IN THE DESERT?

When Jesus was baptised he was filled with God's Spirit.
Jesus had been waiting for this moment for years. Now he was to start preaching. He was to do amazing things to show that God's kingdom had come.

Jesus was a wonderful person. Surely everything would go smoothly?

But the first thing that happened seems very strange. God's Spirit took him out into the desert for forty days. There were no people there. There was no food there. There were wild animals that could attack him.
For forty days, Jesus did not have anything to eat.
Then the Devil came to tempt him.

In the very beginning, when Adam and Eve were living in the beautiful garden surrounded by all the wonderful animals, the Devil tempted them too. They didn't resist him. They sinned.
Later on, when God called his people out of Egypt, they had to go through the desert. They were tempted too. They sinned and failed. They wandered in the desert for forty years. Only two of them were allowed to go into the Promised Land.

Now Jesus was in the desert. The Devil tested him three times.

Jesus must have been very hungry. He was probably feeling very weak.
The Devil said, 'Jesus, you're hungry. Turn some of these stones into bread for yourself. Use the great powers God has given you – if you're really his Son!'
'No' Jesus said, 'God gave me these powers to serve him, not to please myself. We need to obey God's Word even more than we need food!'

So the Devil tried another test. 'The Bible says that God's angels will protect you from harm. Prove it. Jump from the top of the Temple.'
Jesus knew the verse the Devil was talking about. He knew God had promised to protect his people. Jesus trusted God. But the Devil was telling him to test God. He also knew another important Bible verse. He told the Devil: 'The Bible also says "Don't test God."'

At last the Devil showed what he really wanted. He said to Jesus:
'I'll give you the whole world if you'll worship me – just once.'
Jesus had had enough. 'Go away from me, Devil' he said. 'God says that he is the only one who is to be worshipped.'

The Devil left. Because Jesus had trusted God's Word, angels now came to be with him and to keep him company. Perhaps they brought him food as well!

7

Question

What happened to Jesus in the desert?

Answer

Jesus was tested by the Devil, but he said 'no' to all of the Devil's temptations.

Jesus was good. In fact he was perfect. He was holy and he never sinned.

But Jesus was tempted. His temptations didn't come from inside himself. They came from the Devil.

The Devil has been tempting and lying right from the very beginning of the world. He does not like to see people enjoying God's love. He tries to turn us against God.

We sometimes give in. But Jesus did not. The more we say 'no' to the Devil, the harder he tries to trip us up.

Jesus felt the full force of the Devil's temptations when he was hungry and weak. The Devil lied to Jesus.
But Jesus never gave in.

Jesus defeated the Devil. He can help us to say 'no' when we are tempted too.

Memory Verse

Jesus answered, 'It is written: "Man does not live on bread alone, but on every word that comes from the mouth of God." '
Matthew chapter 4, verse 4.

ACTIVITIES

READING TIME

Read Matthew chapter 4, verses 1-11 to discover more about how Jesus was tempted.

TALKING TIME:

Are you ever tempted? How do you think Jesus can help you to be strong?

ACTION TIME:

Ask mum if you can have one of your favourite things to eat. Put it down beside you for one hour. Make sure you can see it. But try not to eat it! Is it easy?
Then, on a piece of paper, draw a calendar with forty-one days. In the first forty spaces write the words: 'Jesus had nothing to eat'. Then in the forty-first space write: 'Jesus defeated the Devil.'  Isn't that amazing when you look at it?

PRAYER TIME:

Lord Jesus, thank you for being so strong when you were tempted. Thank you for defeating the Devil when he tested you. Help me when I am tempted too. And help me to know the Bible the way you did, so that I can get strength from what God teaches me.
Please be with me today. Amen.

JESUS THE GREAT TEACHER

Questions
8 to 14

8. WHAT DID JESUS TEACH THE PEOPLE?

For three years, Jesus went to different towns and villages to preach. Sometimes he went to the great city of Jerusalem and taught there too.

He said that he had come with good news: the kingdom of God had come near.

God's kingdom is not a place, like Great Britain, or Nigeria, or Australia. It is actually much bigger than any place. It contains all the people who love and serve Jesus as King and Lord.

Once when Jesus came back to Nazareth where he had been brought up he was asked to read the Bible lesson in the synagogue. Afterwards he could explain what it meant.
Jesus read from Isaiah chapter 61.

Isaiah had prophesied that someone would come who would be full of God's Spirit. This mysterious person would preach good news. He would set prisoners free. He would make blind people see.

Jesus rolled up the scroll from which he had read. He gave it back to the man who looked after the precious scrolls (ordinary people couldn't afford to have one of their own).
Jesus sat down. Everyone was looking at him. What was going to happen? What would Jesus say?

Jesus spoke. Everyone listened. Jesus said: 'Today Isaiah's promise is being kept.'
The people were totally silent. Did Jesus mean HE was the person Isaiah was speaking about? This was amazing.

The people were really excited. They would have made Jesus king there and then!
But Jesus was not taken in by their excitement. He never is. 'You will turn against me' he said.

Now, instead of welcoming Jesus, the people were angry with him. As quickly as that! In fact they tried to kill him. They did not really want God's kingdom in their lives.

The Devil had left Jesus after the first temptations in the desert. But he had gone away to plot to destroy him some other way. That day he almost succeeded. But God protected Jesus.

Jesus had more to teach the people. But not in Nazareth. Now he went to other places to give his teaching.

Question
What did Jesus teach the people?

Answer
Jesus taught the people about God's kingdom, which is his reign in the hearts of those who belong to him.

Jesus taught in many different places and in many different ways. But his message was always about the same thing: the kingdom of God, or the reign of God, was now beginning.

Jesus himself was the king God had promised to send. When the disciples started following Jesus they became members of his kingdom. As they listened to Jesus they became his disciples or pupils.

Jesus taught them how the kingdom works in this world. He taught them how it would grow. He also taught them that those who belong to his kingdom live different kinds of lives from other people.

We each belong to a country. Our country has its own language and its laws and its customs. We become citizens of that country. But Jesus' followers are citizens in a different kind of country – in Jesus' own kingdom.

In Jesus' kingdom we learn to speak the way Jesus wants us to. We learn to live the way Jesus teaches us. People will begin to notice that we belong to a greater country and a better kingdom. Then they will want to know what kingdom that is. We can tell them: 'It is Jesus' kingdom!'

MemoryVerse:
'The time has come,' Jesus said. 'The kingdom of God is near. Repent and believe the good news!'

Mark chapter 1, verse 15.

ACTIVITIES

READING TIME

The story about how Jesus preached in Nazareth can be found in Luke chapter 4, verses 14-30.

TALKING TIME:
Why do you think it is that people who seem to be enthusiastic about Jesus sometimes turn against him?

ACTION TIME:
Make a scroll today and on it write the words which Jesus read from the Scroll of Isaiah. You'll find them in Isaiah chapter 61, verses 1-2.

PRAYER TIME:
Lord Jesus, you are a wonderful teacher. Help me to learn more about you each time I read my Bible.
Help me to love you always. Keep me from ever turning away from you or against you.
Please help me to show that I belong to your kingdom.
Amen.

9. WHO WERE JESUS' FIRST PUPILS?

Jesus came into the world in order to be our Saviour. God wants all his people to be members of one great big family. So right from the beginning Jesus started to bring his followers together. They were called his 'disciples' which is a word meaning learners or pupils.

Jesus had a plan. First of all he would teach and train a small number of disciples. They would spend lots of time with him and get to know him. Then he would send them out with the message of his love and salvation.

The word used for a person who is sent out by someone else is 'apostle'. Jesus chose twelve men to be his apostles. They would eventually go all over the world to tell other people about Jesus.

But first, Jesus had to call them and to train them.

At least four of the young men Jesus called were fishermen. Do you know their names?
There were two sets of brothers. James and his brother John, and Simon Peter and his brother Andrew. They probably knew each other well.
They had their own fishing business on the Sea of Galilee. They expected to spend the rest of their lives catching fish and then selling them.
But then they heard about Jesus, and listened to his teaching.

One day, Jesus visited them by the seaside. 'Leave your boats and your nets' he said. 'Come with me. I'll help you to "catch" men instead!'
And they did! They told their families what they were going to do. They left everything, and they went with Jesus.

What would these four fishermen have thought of some of the others Jesus called to be with him? They must have been amazed when he called Matthew. They must have known Matthew. He collected taxes from them for the Roman government.
Tax collectors were not liked. They were like traitors. And they made a lot of money.

The fishermen brothers were hard working, honest men. But Jesus chose someone very different to join them. His name was Simon too. He was known as 'The Zealot' because he had wanted to get rid of the Roman soldiers who were in the country – even if he had to kill some of them.

There were others too. One of them was called Judas Iscariot. The others trusted him and made him the disciple-treasurer. But Jesus knew the truth about Judas. He knew Judas would betray him one day.

What an unusual group of men! But only three years later they amazed everybody. They were prepared to go anywhere to tell people about Jesus. They were willing even to die for Jesus, because they loved him so much.

Question
Who were Jesus' first pupils?

Answer
Jesus chose twelve men to be his disciples. He wanted them to be with him, to learn from him and to be sent out by him.

Jesus said that he had come into the world to build a new church. He didn't mean a building. He meant a family of people who trusted and loved him.

In Old Testament times, the church was made up mostly of people who came from the family of Abraham. There were twelve tribes, named after the sons of Abraham's grandson, Jacob.

But they had let God down so badly that God planned to start something new.

Jesus' church was new. And yet he wanted to show that it continued God's true church in the Old Testament.

So, just as the Old Testament church had twelve tribes, Jesus chose twelve men to be his apostles. They were the first building blocks in his church!

Memory Verse
Jesus appointed twelve—designating (calling) them apostles—that they might be with him and that he might send them out to preach and to have authority to drive out demons.

Mark chapter 3, verses 14-15.

ACTIVITIES

READING TIME

To find out the names of all the apostles, read Mark chapter 3, verses 13-19.

TALKING TIME:
Read through the names of the apostles again. Which ones do you think you might not have chosen? Why did Jesus choose them, do you think?

ACTION TIME:
Simon Peter is one of the best known of the disciples. The New Testament says a lot about him.

Using the following passages, make a Fact File of the time in Simon Peter's life he spent with Jesus.

John 1:40-42.
Matthew 4:18-19; 14:29-30; 16: 13-23; 17:1-13; 17:24-27.
John 13:6-17; 18:10-11; 18:25-27.
Matthew 26:75.
John 20:3-8; 21:3-17.

PRAYER TIME:
Lord Jesus, thank you for choosing ordinary people to be your disciples. Thank you for inviting me to follow you. I am very small and weak. I feel I cannot be your disciple in my own strength. Please give me your strength, and help me to serve you well. I trust you and I love you. Thank you for being my Friend. Amen.

10. WHY DID JESUS TELL SO MANY UNUSUAL STORIES?

After Jesus left home, he became a preacher. He went to different places to tell people that God's kingdom was very near. He was the king. And when the king comes, his kingdom comes too!

People loved to listen to Jesus talk. He was different from all the other teachers they had listened to. He was really interesting to listen to.

Boys and girls liked to go into the countryside to listen to Jesus. One boy liked him so much he gave Jesus his own lunch and said 'Please share this with anybody who forgot to bring food.' Jesus shared the bread and fish the boy gave him with five thousand people!

Jesus is king. He wants to be our king.

He told wonderful stories to get people to think about what this means.
His stories are called *parables*.

Parables are stories that have little puzzles hidden inside them.
You have to try to work out what they really mean.

Lots of people loved Jesus' stories. But they didn't really understand them.
Jesus said they listened, but they didn't really hear.
They thought Jesus' stories were great. But they didn't understand that Jesus was talking about them. They forgot to ask: What is Jesus trying to tell me?

Jesus told lots of great stories.
He said that when he taught he was just like a farmer sowing seed in the ground.
Some people have hearts that are like hard ground. Jesus' teaching never gets inside.
Others have hearts that are like ground with hard rock underneath. Jesus' teaching doesn't get very far. Still others have hearts that are like ground full of weeds. Jesus' teaching doesn't last very long.
But some people have hearts that are ready to listen to Jesus and to obey him.

What kind of ground are you?

Sometimes when your face is dirty and your hair is in a mess, mum says to you: 'Go and look in the mirror – see what you're like!'
Jesus' story about the different soils is like a mirror. He is saying: 'What kind of ground are you? What is your heart like?
Do you listen, and understand, and obey my teaching?'

10

Question
Why did Jesus tell so many unusual stories?

Answer
Jesus told stories called parables. They are stories which show us how his kingdom works.

Whenever Jesus taught he used wonderful stories called parables.
He knew people would enjoy them. We all love a good story.

But Jesus wanted people to THINK about what he was saying. So he told stories with hidden meanings. Only those who wanted to learn about him and his kingdom would try to really understand them.

Some of Jesus stories have different kinds of people in them. When you read them, Jesus wants you to ask yourself: 'Which person am I really like?'
When you read the parables, Jesus also wants you to ask: 'What does this story say to me about how God works in his kingdom?'

Jesus' stories are so marvellous you can read them again and again!

MemoryVerse
Jesus told them, 'The secret of the kingdom of God has been given you. But to those on the outside everything is said in parables.'
Mark chapter 4, verse 11.

ACTIVITIES

READING TIME

Read Mark chapter 4, verses 1-20 and you will find out more about Jesus' parables.

TALKING TIME:

Jesus said a very strange thing. He explained the reason why he taught in stories. He told his disciples that they would find the answer in Isaiah chapter 6, verses 9 and 10. Look those verses up in your Bible. Why do you think Jesus told stories?

ACTION TIME:
Sometimes when Jesus taught beside the sea, there were big crowds listening. He got into a boat so everyone could see him. Have you noticed how easily voices travel over water? Everyone could hear him. Can you draw the crowd?

PRAYER TIME:
Lord Jesus, Thank you for being my teacher. You are very wise and loving. Teach me how  to understand what you say. Teach me how to trust you and love you too. Help me to put into practice and obey what you tell me. Amen.

11. WHAT DID JESUS SAY GOD IS LIKE?

Jesus taught the people all about God's kingdom. But something troubled Jesus. He saw that the people didn't really know God as their Heavenly Father. He wanted to help them to trust him and to love him.

A long, long time before Jesus came, something terrible had happened.

Right at the beginning, God had put Adam and Eve in a wonderful garden. It was full of beautiful things. There were rivers and trees with different kinds of fruit. All kinds of wonderful – and friendly – animals were roaming around. It must have been great!

Adam and Eve had God's presence with them. God loved them and said to them: 'You can eat any of the fruits in this garden. It's all for you. But I want you to do one thing, to show that you want to obey me. There is a tree in the middle of the garden. You must not eat its fruit. If you do, we will no longer be able to be friends, and you will die. Do this, just to show me that you trust me and that you want to do what I say.'

But God had an enemy. That enemy became the enemy of Adam and Eve too. He wanted to spoil God's pleasure in having Adam and Eve as his friends. He wanted to spoil Adam and Eve's pleasure in having God as their Heavenly Father and their friend. That enemy was the same one who later tried to tempt Jesus into disobeying God. Remember? He was the Devil, who is sometimes called 'Satan' in the Bible.

The Devil used a snake. Animals have a language of their own, don't they? Dogs bark. Cats meow. Lions growl. Snakes hiss. We know too that some animals can hear things we can't hear. Some animals can hear things a long way away, as if they had a whole telephone system in their ears! Perhaps in those days Adam and Eve could understand what the animals said.

One day they heard the snake saying: 'Don't listen to God. He doesn't really love you at all. He won't let you eat from any of the trees in the garden, will he?'. THAT WAS A HORRIBLE LIE. Adam and Eve should have said, 'You are a horrible cheat and a liar!'
God had given them everything, and told them there was only ONE tree they were not to eat from. But the Devil twisted what God had said. He claimed God had said they were to get nothing. He said that God wasn't really a loving Father at all. Adam and Eve made a terrible mistake. They believed this LIE.

People have been believing that lie ever since. That was why when Jesus taught them, he said: 'I have come into this world so that you might get to know that God wants to be your Heavenly Father.' When Jesus spoke to God he called God his Father

When we belong to Jesus we can call God 'Father' as well. Isn't that wonderful?

Question

What did Jesus say God is like?

Answer

Jesus said that God loves us and wants to be our Heavenly Father.

Lots of people today say that God is a great Heavenly Father.

But just like the people in Jesus' day, they don't really know him or trust him.

When they talk about God, they don't use the word 'Father'.
When they pray, they don't call him 'Our Father'.
They don't live like people who know that the Heavenly Father is watching over them.

That is because in their hearts they think of God the way the Devil made Adam and Eve think about him. And because they have sinned against him (as we all have), they don't trust him.

But when Jesus spoke about God, he called him 'Father'.
He wants us to be able to trust him as our Father too.

Memory Verse

Jesus said, 'No-one knows the Father except the Son (Jesus) and those to whom the Son chooses to reveal him.'
Matthew chapter 11, verse 27.

ACTIVITIES

To find out more about how Adam and Eve came to believe the terrible lie, read Genesis chapter 3, verses 1-13.

TALKING TIME:

What do you usually call God? Do you think you have ever believed the terrible lie about him? Are you trusting him to be your Heavenly Father too?

ACTION TIME:

Draw a picture of what happened to Adam and Eve.

PRAYER TIME:

Lord Jesus, thank you for showing me what God is like. Thank you for telling me that he is a loving Heavenly Father who cares for me very much.
I am really sorry that sometimes I haven't really trusted him. Sometimes I haven't loved him as a Heavenly Father.
Thank you, Jesus, for trusting the Heavenly Father. And thank you for letting us call your Father 'our Father'.
Amen.

12. WHAT DID JESUS SAY ABOUT HOW TO ENTER HIS KINGDOM?

Jesus taught the people that the kingdom of God had come near. He began to teach his disciples that he was the king in God's kingdom. He did wonderful things. And he told marvellous parables about the kind of thing that happens when God's kingdom comes.

One night a man called Nicodemus came to see Jesus. He was famous. Nicodemus was one of the best teachers of the Bible in the whole country.

Maybe he came to see Jesus when it was dark so that nobody would notice him. But he had thought a lot about what Jesus was doing and saying. When he met Jesus he spoke nicely to him – not like some of the other teachers.

'Jesus,' said Nicodemus, 'We know you have come from God. You have said and done wonderful things. So you must have been sent by God.'

Jesus could see right into Nicodemus' heart. He saw that Nicodemus didn't really understand who Jesus was. Nicodemus was very respectful to Jesus as a teacher. Nicodemus thought that Jesus did wonderful things. But he didn't really understand about the kingdom. Jesus said to him: 'Nicodemus, in order to see and enter the kingdom, you need to be born from heaven.'

Poor Nicodemus. He gave himself away. He was supposed to know his Bible really well. But he couldn't understand what Jesus was talking about! He thought he could see things clearly, but he said to Jesus 'Jesus, I don't see what you mean.'
Nicodemus showed by what he said that he really did need to be 'born from heaven.'

But what did Jesus mean? 'How can somebody be born a second time?' asked Nicodemus.
Jesus gave him the answer. We can't really get to know God as our Father unless he sends his Spirit to give us a new heart. Then we will begin to trust him and to love and obey him. We need a new start – and only God can give us that.

That's why Jesus came. He came to die on the cross for us. He rose again and then went back to heaven. Then he sent his Holy Spirit so that his kingdom could begin in the hearts of everyone who trusts him.

Nicodemus went away very puzzled. But he kept thinking about what Jesus said. Later on he came to trust in Jesus and to love him, and he entered the kingdom!

12

Question

What did Jesus say about how to enter his kingdom?

Answer

We enter the kingdom when the Holy Spirit helps us to see who Jesus is, to trust him as our Saviour and to give our lives to him as our Master and Friend.

Lots of people believe that Jesus was a great man and a wonderful teacher. If you ask them, 'How can I enter the Kingdom?' they will say something like this. 'Try to do the best you can.' 'Live a good life'. 'Try to follow the teachings of Jesus.'

Those are all good things to do. Nicodemus, the great teacher who lived at the same times as Jesus had done these things. But he was still outside of the kingdom.

You can do all these things and still not really belong to Jesus.

Here is what Jesus said about entering the kingdom. You need God's Spirit to work in your heart and to change it.

The first sign that God's Spirit has done this for you is that you trust Jesus as your loving Saviour.

Memory Verse

I will give you a new heart and put a new spirit in you.

Ezekiel chapter 36, verse 26

ACTIVITIES

READING TIME

You can read about the talk Jesus had with Nicodemus in John chapter 3, verses 1-16.

TALKING TIME:

Keep John chapter 3 open. Then you try to read the words of Nicodemus, and get mum or dad to say the words of Jesus.

What do you think Nicodemus would have been thinking about when he went away?

ACTION TIME:

Draw a series of cartoon pictures showing Nicodemus coming to visit Jesus. Put in some bubbles with the most important things that Jesus said.

PRAYER TIME:

Lord Jesus, thank you for being so kind and patient with Nicodemus. Thank you for helping him to see what you were talking about.

Lord Jesus, I don't understand everything, but I do want to trust you. I do want to be in your Kingdom. Please help me to trust you and to follow you. Thank you. Amen.

13. HOW CAN WE BECOME FOLLOWERS OF JESUS?

Jesus said to his disciples 'Follow me.' What did they do? They left everything and began to follow Jesus.

Jesus still calls us today to follow him.

When Jesus calls us, he wants us to see what it really means to be his disciple.

Jesus called his disciples in different ways. But he called each of them to receive his forgiveness and to love him with all their hearts. He called James and John, Andrew and Simon Peter from their fishing business. He called Matthew from his tax-collecting job. He called Zacchaeus to take him home for dinner.

One day a very rich young man asked Jesus how he could receive new life. He wanted to know what to do in order to have the wonderful life that only Jesus can give. Jesus saw that he was rich (he could tell from his clothes).

Jesus knew that this young man loved his riches too much. So he said to him 'Go and sell everything you have. Give the money away to people who are poor. Then come and follow me.'

The rich man hadn't expected Jesus to say this. He was a very nice man. But he hadn't really known how much he loved his riches until that moment. His face fell. He said nothing for a minute, and then he turned round and went home. Jesus must have felt very sad indeed. He knew the young rich man had made the wrong decision.

Another time, Jesus freed a poor man from terrible demons. They had made him unhappy and miserable. They had almost completely destroyed his life. But Jesus told the demons to leave him. The man was immediately changed. Instead of being sad he was suddenly full of joy. 'Let me come with you' he said to Jesus. 'I want to be your disciple.'

Jesus was happy that this man wanted to follow him. But Jesus had a different plan for the man. He wanted him to stay where he was! Jesus wanted him to tell his family and his friends about the wonderful things he had done for him.

The next time Jesus came to that part of the country he discovered crowds of people had heard about him. The man with the demons must have told them all about the Lord!

Jesus wants all of us to follow him. He calls us to turn away from everything that is sinful and wrong. That's what he meant when he said 'Repent'.

He also wants us to give our whole lives to him. That's what he meant when he said 'Follow me'. If we do that, Jesus will show us how to be his disciples.

13

Question
How can we become followers of Jesus?

Answer
Jesus calls us to turn away from everything that is sinful, to trust him as our Saviour, and to give our whole lives to him.

Being a follower of Jesus is the most wonderful thing in the world. It means that Jesus will be our Saviour and our Friend.

There are all kinds of things that try to stop us from following Jesus.

Our hearts have got sin in them, and they can turn us away from Jesus. Sometimes we put other things in Jesus' place. We love them more than we love Jesus.

Sometimes we can be afraid of what other people will say about us, or do to us.

Jesus said that if we are going to follow him, we will share in some of his sufferings. He called that 'carrying the cross.'

Jesus promised to be our Friend and Saviour. He knows that it might be hard to be his disciple. But he calls us to be his followers, just as he called James and John and Andrew and Simon Peter.

Jesus says to us: Come and follow me!

MemoryVerse
Jesus said: 'Anyone who does not carry his cross and follow me cannot be my disciple.'
Luke chapter 14, verse 27.

ACTIVITIES

READING TIME

You will find the story of Jesus and the Rich Young Ruler in Luke chapter 18, verses 18-30.

TALKING TIME:
What different things can stop people from becoming disciples of Jesus? Is there something that might stop you following him?

ACTION TIME:
Get a blank sheet of paper and look up in your Bible Luke chapter 18, verses 29 and 30. Now make two columns, one on the left and the other on the right.
In the left hand one, write down all the things Jesus says his disciples sometimes have to do and in the right hand one, write down what Jesus says his disciples receive.
Now, compare the two columns and put a star beside the one that has got most in it.

PRAYER TIME:
Lord Jesus, thank you for calling me to belong to your disciple band. I know that I have a sinful heart. There are lots of things that could stop me from being your disciple. But I do want to follow you. Help me to turn away from everything that could stop me loving you. Thank you for all the good things you have given me. Amen.

14. WHAT DID JESUS SAY WOULD HAPPEN TO HIM?

Jesus always lived in the presence of his Heavenly Father. He knew everything his Father had said in the Bible. It is hard for us to take in, but Jesus may have memorised all the books in what we call the Old Testament!

When Jesus went for walks, or ran on the hills, or sat by the seaside, he thought about what his Father had said.
He also thought a lot about what Isaiah had written.

God had shown Isaiah that someone would come to be the Saviour. Instead of having a sinful heart, he would do everything God said. He would be like a servant. But then God began to show Isaiah something else. This servant would go through awful suffering. He would be bruised; his body would have wounds on it. He would be treated as if he were a terrible sinner. Yet he had never sinned.

People had tried before to guess who this mysterious servant was.

Jesus thought a lot about what God had said. God was saying to him: 'Jesus, you are the Suffering Servant'.

One passage that describes the Servant says that he experienced all of his sufferings because he was taking the place of others. They had sinned and deserved to be punished. He had not sinned. He did not deserve to be punished. But the Servant said to God: 'I will take their punishment. Instead of punishment they can have my blessings.'

Jesus was the Servant. He began to explain this to his disciples. 'I am going to Jerusalem,' he told them. 'I will be arrested and tried. They will beat me up and then they will kill me' he said. 'But later on I will rise again and be with you.'

At the time, the disciples couldn't take in what he said about rising again. They were just too shocked by what Jesus had said. Peter tried to argue with Jesus. But Jesus told him that he was beginning to sound just like the Devil in the desert.

'No,' said Jesus, 'God's Word will come true. You must remember,' he said, 'that I did not come so that others could serve me, but so that I could be the Servant God promised to send.'

After Jesus had told his disciples all this, they knew that he was definitely going to Jerusalem. Only after his resurrection did they really begin to understand why. Then they began to remember that he had told them a lot more about it than they had taken in at the time.

Question

What did Jesus say would happen to him?

Answer

Jesus said that he was the Servant God had promised to send. He would go to Jerusalem and suffer and die. But he would rise again to be our Saviour and Lord.

Jesus knew that God's plan for his life was already described in the Bible. He knew he was the king in God's kingdom.

But Jesus also knew that God's king was to be the Saviour. He would need to suffer for the sins of others. He would receive the punishment they deserved for their sins. They could then ask God to give them everything that Jesus deserved to get.

At first, Jesus was the only one who knew this. But he began to explain this to his disciples. It was hard for them to take in that the person they loved so much was going to suffer. Much later they understood why.

Memory Verse

He was pierced for our transgressions, he was crushed for our iniquities; the punishment that brought us peace was upon him, and by his wounds we are healed.

    Isaiah chapter 53, verse 5.

ACTIVITIES

READING TIME

You can read about the first time Jesus explained what was going to happen to him in Mark chapter 8, verses 31-38.

TALKING TIME:

How do you think the different disciples must have felt when Jesus told them what was going to happen to him? What do you think they thought or said to Jesus?

ACTION TIME:

In Acts 8:26-40 there is a story about someone else who was trying to puzzle out who the servant described by Isaiah really was.
Can you draw some cartoons of what happened? Put what was said in bubbles.

PRAYER TIME:

Lord Jesus, what you did was very hard to do. Thank you that you became the Suffering Servant that Isaiah spoke about. Thank you for loving people so much that you were prepared to take the punishment for their sins.
Lord Jesus, I know I have sinned, and I don't deserve anything you give me. Thank you for suffering so much in order to be such a great Saviour.
Please help me to love you and trust you more.
– Amen.

JESUS THE GREAT SAVIOUR

Questions
15 to 19

15. HOW DID JESUS SHOW HIS POWER OVER NATURE?

Jesus was able to do miracles. One day Jesus, his mother Mary, and the disciples were all together at a wedding. Usually after a wedding there is a celebration – a party. There are lots of nice things to eat and drink.

Nowadays many people go to a hotel for the celebration. But in some places the people do it all by themselves and sometimes the celebrations can go on for days. It was like that when Jesus went to the village of Cana for the wedding. Mary was helping with all the arrangements. Right in the middle of the celebrations, Mary came to Jesus and said: 'Jesus, they've run out of wine, and the celebrations aren't finished!' That was very embarrassing. It made the families feel very ashamed. It certainly was a bad start to a marriage.

Jesus gave his mother a very strange reply. He asked her why she wanted to involve him. He said that his 'time' hadn't come.We don't know what Mary said. But somehow she knew that Jesus could help the bad situation. She told the servants in the house to do whatever Jesus told them.

This was a Jewish family. They often washed all the things they used at home as a sign that they wanted everything they did to be clean for God. So they needed to have a lot of water. They had six great big water containers in the house. These containers could hold more than one hundred gallons of water! Jesus got the servants to fill up the containers with water. Then he told them to dip a small container into the water, fill it up and take it to the man who was organising the celebrations.

When the man tasted the water, it had turned into wine! It tasted really good. In fact it tasted better than any of the wine they'd been drinking before. He thought that was really unusual. If you drink a lot of something you can easily lose your taste for it. So people were usually given good tasting wine first. Then, when they'd lost their sense of taste, they got the not so good wine. By then they couldn't taste the difference!

Jesus did other amazing things like this. Another time he stopped a storm on the Sea of Galilee. Jesus told the storm to be quiet. And everything went calm. Why did Jesus do these things?

Jesus' miracles were all signs – pictures in action. He knew that sin had really spoiled the world. He knew too that there were dark powers in the world trying to destroy his little disciple band. So, when he turned the water into wine he was showing people that he could give them wonderful things that the Jewish religion couldn't. When he stopped the storm drowning his disciples he showed them that he would protect them.

Jesus has this power because he is the one who created the world in the first place. One day, when Jesus reigns everywhere, we will all enjoy celebrating his power and his love. We will be safe and secure for ever.

15

Question
How did Jesus show his power over nature?

Answer
Jesus showed his power over nature by doing wonderful action signs called miracles.

When sin came into the world at the beginning instead of bringing people happiness it destroyed things.
It is as if the world is no longer God's friend. It does not behave as though it were our friend either. Lots of things go wrong.
Jesus came to be our Saviour. He forgives our sins. But he plans to do more than that. He sees that the world has gone wrong. One day Jesus will put the wrong things in the world right again. That is why he is called 'the Saviour of the world'.

In order to show that he is able to do this, Jesus gave little examples of his great power.
It is as if Jesus were saying: 'Look at that! That is just an example of what I can and will do.'
Imagine what it will be like when he uses all his power to change everything and make the whole world better!

Memory Verse
Jesus revealed his glory, and his disciples put their faith in him.
John chapter 2, verse 11.

ACTIVITIES

READING TIME
You can read the wonderful story of how Jesus stopped the storm from drowning the disciples in Mark chapter 4, verses 35-41.

TALKING TIME:

What kinds of things go wrong in the world? What do you think will happen when Jesus puts them right again?

ACTION TIME:
Draw two 'before and after' pictures to show what happened to the disciples in the boat. Picture 1 should show them in the storm; Picture 2 should show them in the calm.

PRAYER TIME:
Lord Jesus, you have great and amazing power. Thank you for telling me in the Bible that you actually created the whole world.
Thank you, too, that you do not use your power to harm me. Thank you that you use it to help me.

I am looking forward to the time when you put everything right again. Until then, help me to trust you. Help me to be sure that you care about me.
Amen.

16.   WHY DID JESUS HEAL SICK PEOPLE?

 One day after Jesus had been to the church service in Capernaum he went home to Simon Peter's house. Peter was married and his wife was looking after her mother who was feeling very sick. When Jesus heard about it, he went to speak to her and he made her better. Even although Jesus healed her at home, within a few hours everybody in Capernaum seemed to have heard about it. They started bringing sick people to Jesus, including people who had all kinds of diseases and illnesses. Jesus healed them all. Wherever Jesus went he healed people.

Jesus loved to heal people who had leprosy. Leprosy is a disease that affects the skin. There are different kinds of skin diseases, and some of them are worse than others. In Bible times several different skin diseases were called leprosy. Two terrible things happened to anyone who had leprosy.

One of the first things that happened was that the lepers could not feel things, like hot and cold. They couldn't feel pain any longer. Imagine what would happen if you accidentally spilled boiling water over your hand but felt nothing. Lepers got burned and damaged themselves in all kinds of other ways. But there was something else. Lepers were not allowed to live with other people. They were kept apart in case other people caught leprosy from them.

Lepers were like walking pictures to the people. God said: 'Look at the poor lepers; don't you see that when you sin that's what you become like in my sight? You are unclean and not fit for my presence.' Lepers rang a bell and shouted 'unclean, unclean' so that people could keep away from them.

But one day a leper came running up to Jesus. He had heard about his power to heal people. He got right down on his knees in front of Jesus and begged him, 'Jesus, if you want to you can make me clean.' Everybody was watching and asking, 'What will Jesus do?' Would he be angry? Would he tell the man to go away? Would he turn away?

Jesus' heart was full of love and pity for the poor leper. He did an absolutely amazing thing. He reached out his own hand and he lovingly touched the leper. The leprosy disappeared. His skin was perfect again. He could feel things. The man was cured. It was as if Jesus' perfect holiness took away the man's disease. Jesus told the cured leper that he was not to go around talking about this. Instead he was to go to the priest, whose job it was to examine him and see if he was healed.

Jesus didn't want to be known as just a great healer. He wanted people to learn that healing someone of leprosy was just a picture of healing someone from sin. But the healed leper didn't understand. He couldn't stop talking about what Jesus had done. The result was that Jesus had to keep out of the town because so many people wanted to see him.

Isn't it strange that Jesus did a wonderful thing for this man, but he didn't do what Jesus asked him to?

Question
Why did Jesus heal sick people?

Answer
Jesus healed people of all kinds of diseases and sicknesses because he loved them and wanted to help them.

Because of sin our world is full of bad and wrong things. One way in which things have gone wrong is that the world is full of disease and sickness and all kinds of illnesses.

Jesus came to be the Saviour. One day he will change everything and make it what God wants it to be again. In order to show us that he can and will do that, Jesus healed people who were sick.
Jesus is God's own Son. He showed that he really cares about what has happened to us. And he showed that he has the power to make things right.

But Jesus also wants us to understand something very important. He is not just someone who can save people from sickness. What he really wants to do is to save us from our sinfulness.

Memory Verse
Wherever Jesus went – into villages, towns or countryside – they placed the sick in the marketplaces . . . and all who touched him were healed.

Mark chapter 6, verse 56.

ACTIVITIES

READING TIME

Jesus could even heal people who couldn't walk. You can read a great story about how Jesus once did this in Mark chapter 2, verses 1-12.

TALKING TIME:
God told the people that leprosy was a kind of picture of sin. Can you think of ways in which leprosy and sin are similar?

ACTION TIME:
In the Old Testament book of Leviticus, in chapters 13 and 14, there are rules about what was to happen to a leper.
Can you make a poster – like those you see in doctors' waiting rooms?
Make a list of the symptoms – the signs that someone has leprosy.
Make a list of 'What to do if you think you have leprosy'. Underneath in large letters write: JESUS CAN HEAL LEPERS!

PRAYER TIME:
Dear Lord Jesus, it is fantastic that you healed these poor lepers. You are so loving, kind and gentle.
Help me to love people who are sick and to care for them, like you did.
I know you want to heal me from something far worse – my sins.
Please forgive me for them and make my heart clean.
Amen.

17. IS JESUS STRONGER THAN THE DEVIL?

Something strange and unusual began to happen in Jesus' country after he was baptised by John in the River Jordan.

The first sign of it was when Jesus was tempted by the Devil in the desert. The Devil tried to stop Jesus doing God's will. Jesus had come to be the king in the new kingdom God was starting. The Devil wanted to destroy that kingdom right at the beginning, and so he attacked the king.

But then other things began to happen almost everywhere Jesus went. He met people whose lives were being destroyed by demons who were servants of the Devil. Sometimes the Bible calls these demons 'unclean spirits' because they made people do and say unclean things.

These demons were like soldiers in the Devil's army. He was trying to attack Jesus in different ways. He was trying to take control of people Jesus wanted to save. So he was placing his army all over the land.

One day Jesus gave his disciples a great promise. 'I am going to build my church' he said. 'And not even the powers of darkness and death will be able to destroy it!'

Jesus defeated the Devil in the desert. But was Jesus strong enough to defeat him day in and day out?

One day, when Jesus was teaching during the church service and the people were all listening, someone started shouting at Jesus. It was a man who had been invaded by one of the demons. The words he shouted out made it clear to everybody that he was being controlled by an evil spirit: 'What do you want with us, Jesus? Have you come to destroy us? I know who you are—you're the Holy One!' The Holy One is a way of talking about God. He is pure and holy. Sin has no place in his presence.

How did the demon know that Jesus had come to destroy its power? Was it because it was an unclean spirit. Did it know, just from Jesus' presence, that this must be the Holy One?

Jesus told the demon 'Quiet! Be silent!' Suddenly the man shook, there was a terrible shriek, and the demon left him.

Every time Jesus met the Devil's soldiers, the demons, he defeated them. Once he saved a man who was full of hundreds of demons. He is stronger than all the demons. He is stronger than the Devil himself. Jesus is the Great Conqueror.

Question
Is Jesus stronger than the Devil?

Answer
Yes, Jesus is stronger than the Devil and was able to defeat his whole army of demons.

The Bible tells us that there has been an invisible battle going on in the world from the beginning of time. The Devil, who was one of God's most wonderful creatures, turned against him. He became a liar and a cheat. He became jealous and wanted to spoil everything God had made.
The Devil told lies about God right from the beginning. But God promised that he would send a Great Conqueror. The Great Conqueror would defeat the Devil.

When Jesus came as the Great Conqueror, the Devil tried everything he could to stop him. He tempted him. He sent his demons to try to stop what Jesus was doing.

But Jesus really is the Great Conqueror. Jesus defeated the Devil. The Lord Jesus is stronger than the Devil.

MemoryVerse
Jesus said, 'I will build my church, and the gates of Hades will not overcome it.'
Matthew chapter 16, verse 18.

ACTIVITIES

Read the amazing story about Jesus' power over the Devil and his demons in Mark chapter 5, verses 1-20.

TALKING TIME:
Try to imagine what it must have been like for the man who called himself Legion. A legion was a part of an army, usually with thousands of soldiers.
What do you think he felt? Do you think he was frightened? Was there anything he could do to save himself? What do you think he felt like after Jesus saved him?

ACTION TIME:
Can you draw some really good cartoon pictures of the story told in Mark's Gospel chapter 5? Make sure you include a picture of what the man did after Jesus had set him free from the demons.

PRAYER TIME:
Dear Lord Jesus, how wonderful it is that you helped the poor man who was really a slave to all those demons. I know the Bible teaches me that sin makes me a slave as well. Please protect me from becoming its slave. And help me to live for you so that others can see the power you have in my life. I love you very much. Amen.

18. CAN JESUS DEFEAT DEATH?

Jesus came into the world to be our Saviour. In order to be our Saviour, Jesus had to save us from everything that spoils and destroys our lives. We know that being sick, or unhappy and lots of other things can make us sad and spoil our lives, but there is something that can totally spoil our lives, isn't there? It is death.

Death is the end of life in this world. You stop breathing, your heart stops beating, your brain stops working. Some people think that's all there is - as if we were just machines that stop working. But God has made us to live for ever. Death is not something that just happens, it is the result of things going wrong in the world. It is the result of sin. Sin leads to separation from God. So, death must be very powerful. But it is not more powerful than Jesus. He is The Great Conqueror. He can beat death and overcome it.

When Jesus spoke to his disciples about his own death, he told them that he would come back to life again. Death seemed to have won the victory over him when he died on the cross. But within three days he overcame its grip and rose again. But how could Jesus get his own disciples to believe he would rise again from the dead? He proved it by bringing people who had died back to life again. Of course, these people would die again later on. So it was a bit different from Jesus' own resurrection. But it did show that he was The Great Conqueror.

Jesus raised three people to life again.

The first person Jesus raised was the twelve year old daughter of a man called Jairus. People laughed at Jesus when he told them that she would be brought back to life. They didn't believe Jesus. But he did it.

The second one was the son of a widow woman in Nain. A widow is someone whose husband has died. You can imagine how special her son was to her. Jesus brought him back to life too.

Jesus didn't know either the little girl or the young man. But later on a man called Lazarus died. He was one of Jesus' best friends. He lived in Bethany near Jerusalem, and Jesus loved spending time in his home. After Lazarus had been dead for several days, Jesus visited his two sisters called Martha and Mary. He told them that Lazarus would rise again.

Jesus visited the grave of Lazarus. It was probably a cave. He told the men to roll away the stone that covered it. Then he shouted out very loudly, ' Lazarus! Come out!'   To everybody's amazement (except Jesus'), Lazarus came staggering out of the tomb! Jesus had raised him from the dead. He proved his power. He proved he was The Great Conqueror.

Not long after that, Jesus was put to death. Then, three days later, he rose again. He really and truly is The Great Conqueror.

18

Question
Can Jesus defeat death?

Answer
Yes, Jesus can defeat death. He proved it by bringing people who were dead back to life. Then he rose again from the dead himself. Jesus is alive for ever.

A Christian can have all kinds of enemies, just as Jesus did.
Sometimes people can be our enemies. They can say and do nasty things to us because we are followers of the Lord Jesus.
The Devil is always our enemy. He tries to draw us away from Jesus. He wants to stop us loving him. He sometimes offers us things we like, in order to tempt us - just like fishermen put bait on their hooks to trap the fish.
We have an enemy in our own hearts – it is called sin.
But there is another enemy we will all meet unless Jesus comes back beforehand. This last enemy is called death. It is a very frightening enemy for some people.
We need to know something very important about this enemy. Jesus overcame it when he rose from the dead!

Memory Verse
Jesus said, 'I am the resurrection and the life. He who believes in me will live, even though he dies.'
John chapter 11, verse 25.

ACTIVITIES

READING TIME

You will find the whole story about the daughter of Jairus in Mark chapter 5, verses 21-24 and 35-43.

TALKING TIME:
Why do you think it is that grown ups don't like talking about death? What do you think makes people frightened of death? What difference would it make to them if they knew that Jesus is a risen Saviour?

ACTION TIME:

Draw a picture of something that frightens you - perhaps it might be a spider or maybe you don't like snakes?
Then look up Psalm 56, verse 3 and write it out underneath your picture to remind you to trust Jesus whenever you're afraid.

PRAYER TIME:
Lord Jesus, I want to thank you that you met and defeated all my enemies. You are The Great Conqueror. I am glad that you are my friend and my Lord.
Lord Jesus, there are still lots of things that make me afraid. Help me to know that if you are with me I do not need to fear any evil.
Amen.

19. HOW DID JESUS SHOW THE DISCIPLES WHO HE REALLY IS?

Jesus and his disciples were together for three years. Sometimes the disciples thought they really loved Jesus. They felt that they knew him very, very well. But at other times they didn't seem to be able to understand him. They found it difficult to accept what he said.

One day Jesus told them that he was going to die on the cross. Simon Peter didn't like that. He began to argue with Jesus. He took hold of him and said that he must never let that happen. But Peter was wrong. He didn't really understand who Jesus was. Jesus was the Son of God. Peter had said to Jesus that he knew that. But he didn't understand.

One day Jesus took Peter and James and John with him on a hike. They climbed up a mountain together. They must have been wondering why Jesus was taking them up the mountain. He wanted them to see something. At the top of the mountain they sat down to rest. Peter, James and John were beginning to feel quite sleepy up at the top of the mountain. They didn't talk, they were so tired. When Jesus saw they were sleepy, he used the time of quiet to talk to his Father in heaven.

Something amazing happened while he was praying. His face seemed to change, and he was shining. We don't know how often this happened to Jesus. But something else happened. Moses and Elijah suddenly appeared and started talking to Jesus about what he was going to do in Jerusalem. Moses was the man God used to give the Law to his people. Elijah was the great prophet God used to tell the people what God wanted. And now they were visiting Jesus. They seemed to be just alive with light. They were talking to Jesus about his death.

The talking woke up Peter, James and John. They couldn't believe their eyes. There was Moses and Elijah – it couldn't be anyone else. And there was Jesus like they had never seen him before. It was as though the glory of God was shining out from inside him.   Peter was excited and afraid at the same time. Just like Peter – he felt he needed to say something and do something. 'Let's build three shelters, Jesus' he said – 'one for you, another for Moses and another for Elijah.'

Peter didn't really understand what was going on. Just as he was speaking, a cloud covered the top of the mountain. It was a very strange experience. It was very bright, but it was also very thick; they couldn't see anything. From right inside the cloud a voice spoke. It was the voice of God. It said: 'Peter, James, John – Listen! Jesus is my Son. I have chosen him. Listen to him. Listen to what he has to say. Trust him; do what he says.'

Peter, James, and John kept all this to themselves. They didn't let anyone know what had happened until after Jesus was raised from the dead. But they knew what had happened. They knew that they had been allowed to see who Jesus really is. He is the Son of God.

19

Question

How did Jesus show the disciples who he really is?

Answer

Jesus took Peter, James, and John with him up a mountain where he let them see the glory of God in his life.

The Bible speaks about something called the 'glory' of God.
When God shows his glory, it is as if he shows us everything that he is all at once. Because he is invisible and we can't see him, he helps us by showing us his glory in ways we can see.

God shows us his glory in lots of different ways. God has made the stars and the planets. He made all the wonderful things here on earth as pictures of his amazing power and love. We look at them and think: 'Wow! If God made this he really is amazing!'

Sometimes God wanted his people to see how pure and holy he is. He showed them a bright cloud of light. It was almost as if God himself was inside it, shining through it.
When the disciples were with Jesus on the mountain, God's glory seemed to shine out from within him. And then God's cloud of glory surrounded them and God spoke to them.
God said; 'Jesus is my Son.'

Memory Verse

As Jesus was praying, the appearance of his face changed, and his clothes became as bright as a flash of lightning . . . A voice came from the cloud, saying, 'This is my Son, whom I have chosen; listen to him.'
Luke chapter 9, verses 29, 35.

ACTIVITIES

READING TIME

You can read all about this amazing experience in Mark's Gospel, chapter 9, verses 2-10.

TALKING TIME:
Imagine Peter, James and John talking about seeing Jesus on the mountain top. What would they have said to each other later on that day?

ACTION TIME:
Draw three cartoon pictures, with words in bubbles. Picture one should have the three disciples going up the mountain.

Picture two should show them all as the cloud came down. (How many people were there?)
Picture three should show the disciples talking later on that day.

PRAYER TIME:
Lord Jesus, it is wonderful to think that you showed your glory to your special friends. I would love to be able to see that too. Thank you for promising me that every one who trusts in you will one day see your wonderful, shining glory.
Please help me to live each day for you. And at the end of my life, please bring me right into your presence to see your glory. I love you very much.
Amen.

JESUS GOES TO THE CROSS

Questions
20 to 27

20. HOW MUCH DID JESUS LOVE HIS DISCIPLES?

Jesus had twelve disciples who were called apostles. Wherever Jesus went to teach, they went with him. They heard his parables. They saw his wonderful miracles. But they also spent a lot of time with Jesus on their own – just the small group of them. Then he taught them even more.

One day, after they had listened to Jesus pray, one of them said, 'Jesus, can you teach us a prayer?' Here is the prayer he taught them:

Our Father in heaven,
may your name be special like no other one!
Please build your kingdom.
I ask for your will to be done here on earth
- just as it is in heaven.
Please give me what I need today.
Please forgive my sins
- just as I want to forgive people who do bad things to me.
Please don't let me be tested more than I can stand.
Please save me from anything that is evil.

Jesus loved his disciples a lot. He had come into the world to be their Saviour. In fact he loved them so much that he planned to go to Jerusalem and to die for them there.
Jesus wanted the disciples to know how very much he loved them. Just before the time had come for him to die, he showed them how much he loved them.

It was Passover time. That was the time when the people celebrated how God had set his people free from their slavery in Egypt. That night they had sacrificed a lamb and put its blood outside their tents. The Angel of Death had passed over their tents, and nobody inside was killed. The people had eaten the lamb and other food and then they had left Egypt. Every year the people remembered how God had saved them. They had a meal together, and ate the same things the people had eaten in their tents. Jesus had made arrangements to have a Passover meal with his disciples.

The disciples had all been outside. Their feet were all dirty. The water was all ready there for someone to wash their feet and make them feel clean and cool again. But nobody did it. They all sat down for the dinner with dirty feet. Just when the food started arriving, Jesus got up from the table. Everybody in the room watched him. He took off his robe. He wrapped a long towel round his waist. He looked like a servant. Then he got down on his knees in front of each of the disciples, and he washed their feet clean. He even did it for Judas. Judas was the disciple who was just about to betray him.

When Jesus had finished, he went back to his place at the table. The disciples never forgot that night. Jesus showed them how much he loved them. They remembered how he said 'I did not come to be served, but to serve, and to give my life like a Passover Lamb to set you free from sin.'

20

Question

How much did Jesus love his disciples?

Answer

Jesus loved his disciples so much that he was willing to die for them. One night he showed them how he had come down from heaven to die on the cross so that their sins could be washed away. He got up from the table, knelt down in front of them and washed their dirty feet.

Jesus was full of love for his disciples. He looked after them while they were all together. He taught them about the love of the Heavenly Father. He was very kind to them. He was very patient with them. Sometimes that must have been very difficult. They made mistakes. They didn't always understand what he was saying. Sometimes they argued with each other. At other times they didn't really trust him.

On the night on which Jesus was arrested he washed his disciples' feet. They never forgot it.

Afterwards Jesus told them that they were to follow his example. He didn't mean that they should wash each other's feet all the time. He meant that they should love each other and care for each other just as he had done for them.

Jesus said that showing this love is the sign that we love him. It is the sign that we are true disciples.

MemoryVerse

Jesus said: 'Now that I, your Lord and Teacher, have washed your feet, you also should wash one another's feet.'
John chapter 13, verse 14.

ACTIVITIES

READING TIME

You will find the story of how Jesus washed the feet of his disciples in John chapter 13, verses 1-17.

TALKING TIME:

In most countries today we don't need to wash each other's feet. But what can you do for other people you know to show Jesus' love?

ACTION TIME:

Ask mum to help you fill a basin of water. Ask her for a great big towel. Wrap it round yourself and then kneel down and wash her feet. Imagine doing that twelve times for disciples with very dirty feet.

Is there someone you know to whom you can show this love of Jesus? How will you do that?

PRAYER TIME:

Lord Jesus, thank you so much for washing the feet of the disciples. Thank you for showing them your love in that special way. And thank you even more for dying for us.
Help me to show your love for others by loving them and helping them.
Amen.

21. WHAT DID JESUS PROMISE TO GIVE TO HIS FOLLOWERS?

Jesus made lots of promises to his disciples. Some of them were promises that made them feel very sad. The promise that made them saddest of all was when he said that he would be crucified. That means being put to death by being nailed to a cross.

But Jesus also promised that after he had died he would rise again. He would come back to life and they would see him again.

Jesus made another wonderful promise. He told the disciples that he would send them a very special gift. He would send them this gift after he finally went back to heaven to be with his Father.

There is only one God. But God exists in three persons. He is three in one. Even grown-ups can't really understand that. Only God himself knows what he is like.

Long before the world was made, there was God the Father, his Son, and the Holy Spirit. God lived in a wonderful world of his own. The Holy Spirit was with the Father and the Son. The Holy Spirit loves the Father very much and the Father loves him. The Holy Spirit also loves the Son very much. And the Son loves him too.

So, when the Son came to earth, the Holy Spirit wanted to be near him and with him all the time. Right from the beginning of Jesus' life, the Holy Spirit was like a close friend to him. Although he was invisible, he was always with Jesus.

When Jesus was baptised, the Holy Spirit filled Jesus with power. Then, the Holy Spirit led Jesus out into the Desert to go through the terrible temptations. He gave Jesus power to do miracles. He gave Jesus strength to go to the cross.

After Jesus died, the Holy Spirit gave Jesus new life. The Holy Spirit was at Jesus' side all the time. He saw everything that Jesus went through.

Jesus promised his disciples a very special gift. What do you think Jesus' special gift to his disciples was? The Holy Spirit! Jesus said, 'The Holy Spirit was like my best friend all through my life. I want him to be like your best friend too. So when I leave you, I will send my best friend in my place to be with you.'

Jesus sends the Holy Spirit to every single one of his disciples. When he comes it is just like having Jesus himself with us.

The Holy Spirit comes to live in us to help us to be more like Jesus.

21

Question
What did Jesus promise to give his followers?

Answer
Jesus promised to give his Holy Spirit to his followers. The Holy Spirit is like Jesus' best friend.
He becomes our best friend too.

Before Jesus finally went back to his Father, he told his followers to stay together in Jerusalem.
They did what Jesus told them.

There was a feast in Jerusalem called Pentecost. The city was full of visitors.
The disciples were all gathered together when suddenly they heard a noise. It sounded like a great wind.
It filled the house where they were all sitting together. Then they saw what looked like fiery tongues. Each of them felt the fire coming on them.
What could these strange signs mean?
The Bible words for wind are the same as the Bible words for the Holy Spirit! The wind was a sign of the Spirit.

John the Baptist had said Jesus would baptise his followers with the fire of the Spirit rather than just with water!
That was what Jesus was doing. That's what was happening! Jesus was keeping his promise. He was sending his Spirit!

Memory Verse
Jesus said, 'If you then, though you are evil, know how to give good gifts to your children, how much more will your Father in heaven give the Holy Spirit to those who ask him.'
Luke chapter 11, verse 13.

ACTIVITIES

READING TIME

You can read all about Jesus' promise to send his best friend, the Holy Spirit, in John, chapter 14, verses 15-27.

TALKING TIME:
We all need the strength and power of the Holy Spirit to help us to live for Jesus. Are there special ways in which you should ask the Holy Spirit to help you become more like Jesus?

ACTION TIME:
Pretend it's a very windy day and give a weather report on what has happened because of the strong winds. Then read John chapter 3, verse 8 and remember that the Holy Spirit is like the wind - you can't see him but you can see his power in peoples lives.

PRAYER TIME:
Lord Jesus, I am so glad that when you came into the world you were not alone. It is wonderful to know that you had your best friend with you.
Thank you so much for sharing your best friend with me. Please fill my life with your Holy Spirit. Make me more like you each day.
Thank you for all your good gifts.
Amen.

22. HOW COULD ANYONE BETRAY JESUS?

It is very hard to understand how anyone could have wanted to let Jesus down, isn't it?

Jesus had chosen twelve disciples. He had loved them. He has taken them with him to watch him do all his miracles. They had heard him teaching the great crowds of people. Jesus had taught them as his special friends as well. Don't you think it would have been absolutely amazing to have been with Jesus like that for three years?

One of Jesus' disciples was called Judas Iscariot. Iscariot probably means 'The man from Kerioth.'

All the disciples knew Judas well – they thought. In fact they trusted him a lot. They even made him the disciple who would look after the money they used to buy food and other things when they were travelling around the country. And Judas sounded as though he could be trusted.

One day a woman poured ointment over Jesus' feet to thank him for what he had done. Judas complained. He said it would have been better if the ointment had been sold. They could have given the money to poor people. That sounded as though he really cared about the disciples' money and about the poor. But it really meant that he had stopped loving Jesus. When he saw someone else loving and thanking Jesus he got angry inside.

And there was something else. When nobody was looking, Judas was doing something terrible. He was taking money out of the bag where he kept the disciples' savings. He was stealing from his closest friends. Isn't that horrible? Judas loved money more than he loved Jesus. He knew there were other people who hated Jesus and wanted to kill him. He went to speak to them. They said they would give him money if he took them to some quiet place where Jesus would be. Judas agreed. Judas sinned.

Remember how the Devil had tried to stop Jesus? Now he had found somebody he could use to help him do that. Judas! Judas thought nobody else knew. But Jesus could see right into his heart.

Can you imagine what Judas thought when Jesus lovingly washed his feet before the meal that night? At the meal, Jesus told his friends that one of them was going to betray him. They couldn't believe it. Then Jesus handed Judas some bread dipped in a special sauce. 'Whatever you need to do, do it quickly' he said.

Judas knew Jesus would go out after dinner to the Garden of Gethsemane. He took soldiers there. He went up to Jesus and kissed him. That was the sign he had arranged beforehand with the soldiers. They knew that the person he kissed was Jesus.
The soldiers took Jesus away. They did cruel things to him.

It is hard to understand how Judas could have done what he did. But when we look into our own hearts we know that we let Jesus down too.

22

Question

How could anyone betray Jesus?

Answer

Judas Iscariot betrayed Jesus. He began to love money more than he loved the Master. Then the Devil used him to betray Jesus.

Sometimes we are tempted to do just one thing that we know is against God's will. Nobody else will ever know. We give in and we do it. That was what happened to Judas.

What Judas didn't see was that even a small temptation is like the bait on a fish hook. If the fish swallows the bait, it gets the hook stuck in its mouth and it can't escape.

Judas chose money instead of Jesus. Then he wanted more money. Then he began to love Jesus less and less. And then he began to hate Jesus. He wanted somehow to get Jesus out of his life.

The Devil made sure that Judas got the opportunity to do exactly that. Judas had swallowed the bait. Now he was trapped forever. Later Judas realised what he had done. The Devil didn't care about him then. Judas lost all hope.

Simon Peter let Jesus down the very same night. He said he didn't know Jesus. But he asked Jesus to forgive him. And Jesus did.

It is very important to remember what Jesus said. 'No matter what sin you commit against me, I will forgive it if you ask me.'

Memory Verse

Jesus was troubled in spirit and testified, 'I tell you the truth, one of you is going to betray me.'

John chapter 13, verse 21.

ACTIVITIES

READING TIME

To find out more about what Judas did, read Mark chapter 13, verses 17-21 and 43-50.

TALKING TIME:

How do you think Jesus knew that Judas had stopped loving him? What kinds of things could be used as 'bait' to draw you away from loving and obeying the Lord Jesus? What should we do whenever we fail Jesus?

ACTION TIME:

Make a fact file for the life of Judas Iscariot by using these passages in the Bible:

Mark 3:13-19
John 6:70-71
John 12:1-8
Mark 14:10-11
John 13:1-31
John 18:1-9, Matthew 27:1-10,
Acts 1:12-20

PRAYER TIME:

Dear Lord Jesus, it must have been terrible for you to know that one of your own disciples would betray you. Now I know that you can understand how I feel when people let me down. Thank you for being willing to suffer so much for me. Please help me never ever to

betray you. Please protect me from everything the Devil does to stop me loving you.

I do love you and trust you. Amen.

23. DID JESUS SUFFER A LOT?

Judas Iscariot betrayed Jesus at Passover time. All the people were getting ready to have their special Passover dinner - they did this every year to remember how God had saved them from Egypt. They ate lamb at the dinner, to remind them of the night when the people had put the blood of a lamb on the outside of their houses to protect them from the Angel of Death.

At the dinner, Jesus told his disciples that the first passover lamb was really a picture of himself. He was the Real Lamb. He was going to suffer and die for them. It was his body - not a lamb's - that would be broken for them. His blood - not the lamb's - would be spilt to save them. The disciples still could not take in what Jesus was saying. It seemed impossible. Jesus said that one of them would betray him. How could that happen? He also told Simon Peter that he would deny him. Peter, of all people, deny Jesus? Surely not.

The disciples didn't like the idea of Jesus having to suffer. But Jesus suffered a lot. He knew he was going to suffer. After the dinner, he went to the Garden of Gethsemane. There he began to pray. He asked his Father if there was any other way for him to be the Saviour. 'If this is the only way, Father' he said, 'I'll do it.' When Judas came to kiss him, he brought soldiers. They arrested Jesus and dragged him away to a meeting which the High Priest, the chief priests and the religious leaders had planned. Peter followed at a safe distance. Later on he was able to tell people what had happened.

The priests had got people to come and to lie about Jesus, while Jesus just stood there. The High Priest got so angry that he shouted out: 'Are you the Son of God?'
'Yes I am,' Jesus replied.   Then the High Priest really lost his temper and tore his robes. 'You're speaking against God,' he said 'this is blasphemy.' Some of them began to spit on Jesus and to laugh at him. The guards took him away and beat him up. Then they tied Jesus up again, and took him to see Pontius Pilate who was the Roman Governor.

Pilate talked with Jesus. He knew that Jesus had done nothing wrong. So he told the people that Jesus hadn't done anything against the Roman Emperor. But they shouted out 'Crucify him!' again and again. They wanted Jesus to be put to death by being nailed to a wooden cross and left there to die. They said, 'We'd rather have Barabbas than Jesus of Nazareth.' The people knew that Pilate always let one prisoner go free every Passover time. Barabbas was a murderer. He was set free.

The soldiers took Jesus away. They began to beat him with wooden rods. Sometimes prisoners died from these beatings. The soldiers were very cruel and started making fun of Jesus. They kept on hitting him on the head with a piece of wood. They pressed a crown made of thorns on him. It must have been awful.Then the soldiers made Jesus carry the wooden cross on which he was going to be crucified. Jesus was so weak he couldn't carry it. They made a man who was passing by carry it. His name was Simon.
Eventually they got Jesus to a place that was called Golgotha. They hammered nails through his hands and his feet right into the wood. Then they raised the cross up. People were laughing. Some people were shouting at him.

It was terrible. But Jesus went through all that suffering because he loves us.

23

Question
Did Jesus suffer a lot?

Answer
Jesus suffered by being beaten, spat upon and laughed at. Then he was crucified. He died a cruel and terrible death in our place.

Jesus suffered a lot. His disciples ran away and he was left all on his own. His body was really beaten up. Nobody came to help him. Nobody said 'stop it' to the people who were torturing him.

The religious leaders had this all planned. They probably invited only some of the leaders to take part in their meeting. They knew that someone like Nicodemus – who had once visited Jesus-would not like what they did.

Jesus must have been very, very sore and very weak. His body would have been covered in cuts and blood. But even when he was on the cross, he prayed. He asked God to forgive the people.
Jesus' prayer was answered even when he was on the cross. A criminal who was being crucified beside him asked Jesus for forgiveness. He asked to be in Jesus' kingdom!

Jesus began to feel as if God had turned his back on him too. At one point he cried out, 'My God, why have you left me?' That was because he was taking the place of sinners. That was the worst suffering of all.

Jesus went through it to be our Saviour.

Memory Verse
He poured out his life unto death, and was numbered with the transgressors. For he bore the sin of many, and made intercession for the transgressors.

Isaiah chapter 53, verse 12

ACTIVITIES

READING TIME

You can read part of the story of Jesus' crucifixion in Luke chapter 23, verses 26-49.

TALKING TIME:

What different thoughts do you think must have been passing through Jesus' mind on the day he was crucified?

ACTION TIME:
Look at the front page of a newspaper and notice how it describes things that happen in the world. Think of what headline you would use and then try to write your own front page of *The Jerusalem Times* for the day that Jesus was crucified.

PRAYER TIME:
Lord Jesus, I do not like to think about pain and suffering. I cannot really begin to take in that you suffered so much for me. How could you love me so much that you would be willing to do that? What can I say to you but 'Thank-you, Dear Lord'? I ask you to help me to understand and feel how much you love me. Amen.

24. WHY DID JESUS HAVE TO DIE?

Jesus went through terrible suffering on the cross. When he spoke about it, both before and afterwards, he always said that he *had* to do it. But why did he *have* to suffer?

Do you remember the time when Jesus came to the River Jordan where John was baptising? When John recognised who Jesus really was he said: 'Look, this is the Lamb of God who will take away the sins of the world.' What did he mean?

Long before the days of Jesus, God said to Abraham: 'Abraham, take Isaac and sacrifice him to me on the mountain.' Abraham was shocked. He must have been very frightened. He was an old man when Isaac was born. He loved him very, very much. How could God ask him to do this? But Abraham wanted to do what God told him—even if he couldn't understand. So he got Isaac up early in the morning. They travelled by donkey for three days until they reached the mountain God had told him about.

Abraham and Isaac went on their own up the mountain. Abraham was old, and found it difficult to climb. Isaac carried all the things they needed. He had told Isaac that they were going to the top of the mountain to offer a sacrifice to God. But Abraham hadn't told Isaac what the sacrifice was going to be.

Isaac was carrying wood, and something to light the sacrificial fire with. Isaac was also carrying a big knife. They would need a big knife to kill the animal for the sacrifice. But there was something missing. Isaac was puzzled. 'Father?' said Isaac. 'Yes, Isaac?' Abraham replied. 'Father, we have got the wood, and we can light a fire. I have the knife. But where is the lamb for the sacrifice?'

Can you imagine how Abraham must have felt? What could he say? Suddenly he thought of something that was true—but meant he could still keep the terrible secret from Isaac. 'God himself will provide a lamb,' he replied.

When they reached the top, Abraham must have explained what was going to happen. He tied Isaac up on top of the wood. Isaac must have been willing to die. He was far stronger than his father Abraham. He could have stopped him. Abraham held the knife in his hand. He lifted it up slowly, because he was going to sacrifice his own son. Suddenly God's angel stopped him! Abraham looked round. He saw a ram in the bushes. Abraham untied Isaac, and he sacrificed the ram instead. God wanted to teach Abraham and all the people after him a very important lesson about Jesus. It was this:

We have all done wrong things and sinned against God. We all deserve to die for our sins. But God promised that he would provide the sacrifice that would take our place.

Abraham's words were true, after all. Eventually God did provide a lamb that would be sacrificed instead of us. Jesus is the Lamb of God who takes away our sins. That is why Jesus had to die.

24

Question

Why did Jesus have to die?

Answer

Jesus had to die because he was the Lamb that God had promised. He was like the Passover lamb who died to protect the people from God's judgement on Egypt. When Jesus died he took the punishment for our sins.

God had an amazing plan. The whole world had turned away from him. The people in the world became enemies. They didn't love God and they tried to destroy what he did.

Everyone who turns away from God deserves to be punished.
But God wanted to save the world.

God had already decided the only way this could be done. He would send his only Son to die in our place.
God had to get everything ready and in place for Jesus to come. But he wanted the people who lived before Jesus to know something about him, and to trust in him. So he arranged things to help them to understand what he would do.

What happened to Isaac was one of those things. Abraham was going to sacrifice his son. But God stopped him at the last minute. He didn't need to. God was going to sacrifice his Son instead.

Memory Verse:

He who did not spare his own Son, but gave him up for us all – how will he not also, along with him, graciously give us all things?
Romans chapter 8, verse 32.

ACTIVITIES

READING TIME

You can read all about what Abraham did in Genesis chapter 22, verses 1-19.

TALKING TIME:

How do you think Abraham must have felt on the journey he made to the mountain?

How would God the Father have felt when Jesus went to the cross?

ACTION TIME:

Pretend you are Abraham and ask your mum or dad to interview you for the 'Jerusalem Television News.'

Get them to ask you about what happened and how you felt when you took Isaac up the mountain.

PRAYER TIME:

Lord Jesus, I don't suppose I will ever understand all that you suffered. Thank you for showing me in the Bible why you died. Thank you that when your Heavenly Father led you to the cross you were willing to go.
Thank you for being willing to be my Saviour. Help me always to trust you. And help me to love you more and more.
Amen.

25. IS JESUS STILL DEAD?

Jesus died on the cross in the afternoon. Before he died he said something in a very loud voice. People were surprised by how strong it was, because he must have been very, very weak. They were also puzzled by what he said. It sounded like a shout of triumph and victory. He shouted out: 'It's finished!'

Jesus had finished doing everything his Father had wanted him to do. So he bowed his head and he asked his Father to take care of him. Then something really wonderful happened.

The Romans didn't allow criminals to be buried. And the Jews didn't allow the body of someone who had been crucified to be buried in the family grave. What was going to happen to the body of Jesus? That afternoon two men went to see Pilate. They said to him: 'Please let us take Jesus' body down from the cross and bury it.' Pilate didn't really care now about Jesus. So he said they could do it.

The name of one of the men was Joseph. He was one of the Jewish leaders, but he hadn't been asked to go to the meeting when Jesus was tried and beaten up. They must have known he would have tried to stop that. Joseph was a rich man. He owned a tomb in a nice garden. He had probably bought it for his family. It had never been used. He must have loved Jesus because he was willing to have Jesus buried in his own family grave.

Can you guess the name of the other man?   It was Nicodemus. He must have begun to trust and love Jesus too. These two men carefully took Jesus' body down from the cross and carried it to the garden tomb. They buried Jesus in the tomb. They got help to roll a great stone over the front.

The next day was the Jewish holy day. All through that day Jesus' body lay still and silent in the tomb. Nobody came to visit it. But early the next morning something absolutely amazing happened to Jesus' body. His spirit came back to it. His body came back to life and now it had great new powers. Jesus got up, just as if his body had been asleep. He took off the cloths that had been wrapped round his dead body.

Guards had been posted near the tomb to make sure nobody stole Jesus' body and then pretended that he had kept his word about rising from the dead. They heard a tremendous rumble. It was a kind of earthquake. They didn't know what was going on inside the tomb. An angel came from heaven. He was so bright that it was as if there had been a tremendous flash of lightning. The guards ran for their lives.

Then, when nobody else was there, the angel rolled away the great stone in front of the tomb. What do you think the angel would have said to Jesus?

Jesus walked right out of the tomb. Jesus is still alive!

25

Question

Is Jesus still dead?

Answer

No! Jesus really did die on the cross, and then his body was buried nearby in a tomb in a garden. But two days later he came back to life and is alive now forever.

Jesus really did die. Then he was buried. The Bible tells us that the cause of death is sin. Death came into the world because of sin. That is why we all die. Sin puts seeds of death into our lives.
But Jesus did not sin. No seeds of death could grow in him.

God's plan was that Jesus would take our place. Jesus would die instead of us. He would take the punishment for sin.
Otherwise Jesus would never have died.
Death is strong enough to keep hold of sinful people. But it doesn't have the strength to keep hold of a really good and perfect person. It wasn't strong enough to keep Jesus a prisoner for more than a couple of days. Jesus just snapped the ropes death had used to tie him up.

When Jesus walked out of the garden tomb, he left death behind. Death fell to pieces.
Because Jesus defeated death for himself, we know that he'll do it for us some day too.

Memory Verse

God raised Jesus from the dead, freeing him from the agony of death, because it was impossible for death to keep its hold on him.

Acts chapter 2, verse 24.

ACTIVITIES

READING TIME

The story of Jesus' resurrection is told in each of the four Gospels. You can read it in Matthew chapter 27, verse 57 to chapter 28 verse 15.

TALKING TIME

What do you think the disciples must have felt like after Jesus had died? You'll get some clues in Mark chapter 16, verses 1-3 and in Luke chapter 24, verses 13-18.

ACTION TIME:

Pretend that you were one of the guards who had kept watch at Jesus' tomb. Write a report for your commander, telling him what you saw and heard and how you felt.

PRAYER TIME:

Lord Jesus, it is absolutely marvellous that you defeated the power of death. You are great and strong. Thank you so much for coming back to life and showing your disciples that you keep all of your promises.

And thank you too that you are still alive. Thank you for being with me as my Saviour and my Friend. You are a wonderful Saviour and I want to praise you.
Amen.

26. WHAT IS JESUS DOING NOW?

After he had risen from the dead, Jesus stayed with his disciples for about six weeks. He helped them to understand better what he had already taught them. He told them more about his kingdom. He prepared them for the time when he would leave them and go back to Heaven.

When that day came, Jesus took them to a quiet place. He broke the news to them that this was their last day together. One day they would all be together again – forever! But today he was going back to his Father. They were to go back to Jerusalem. In Jerusalem the Holy Spirit would come to them. He would help them to tell others there about Jesus. And then he would take them all over the world, telling people about Jesus.

Remember when Peter, James and John were with Jesus on the mountain and the bright cloud came down? It happened again on this day too. Jesus just seemed to disappear in the cloud. It must have been an amazing experience for the disciples.

The disciples did what Jesus told them to do. Everything he said turned out just the way he told them. They went all over the place telling people about their Lord Jesus. Some of them were very badly treated because they were Jesus' disciples. Some of them were killed. But their message about Jesus spread. In fact, it spread all over the world until it came to the country you live in too.

But what did Jesus do after he left his disciples? Jesus went back to Heaven. Can you imagine the welcome he got there? He is the king of the angels as well as being our king. They must have been really excited. It must have been the greatest thing they had ever seen. They had watched everything he did. Sometimes the Father had sent one of them to be with Jesus. But now all of them could cheer him. Jesus took his place beside his Father.

But what is Jesus doing now? He is looking after the whole world, so that God's plan for it will be worked out. Jesus keeps everything going. Jesus is also looking after his people in a special way. He has given us the part of the Bible we call The New Testament. It tells us all about Jesus and what his will is. Jesus sends the Holy Spirit to help us to understand it.

Jesus still calls us to be his disciples. We don't hear his voice the way Andrew, Simon Peter, James and John did. But he uses his Word, the Bible, to speak to us. He speaks right into our hearts, and we know that he is calling us to follow him.

Jesus said to his disciples: 'I am going to build my church, and nothing will stop me.' Right down through the centuries, Jesus has been doing this. Nothing can ever stop him.

Isn't that good news?

26

Question

What is Jesus doing now?

Answer

Jesus keeps the whole world going. Everything depends on his power. He does this because he wants to build his church all over the world.

Jesus said that he had come into the world in order to build his church. When he left the disciples he sent his Holy Spirit to take his place. The Holy Spirit then sent Jesus' disciples all over the world with the good news about Jesus.

Sometimes the church has been attacked. Sometimes it has become very weak. In some countries it sometimes almost disappears.

And sometimes Christians aren't very good at doing what Jesus tells them. Sometimes they haven't cared as much as they should about telling the whole world about Jesus.

But Jesus always looks after his church. Jesus has called different people to go to all the different countries to tell the boys and girls and grown-ups the good news.

One day Jesus will finish building his church. Then he will come back again. Then the first disciples – and all the disciples since – will be together with him for ever.

Memory Verse

Jesus said, 'Go and make disciples of all nations . . . And surely I am with you always, to the very end of the age.'
   Matthew chapter 28, verses 19 and 20.

ACTIVITIES

READING TIME

You can read about Jesus' last days with his disciples in Acts chapter 1, verses 1-12.

TALKING TIME:

Imagine you were with Simon Peter, Andrew, James and John on the way back to Jerusalem after Jesus had gone back to heaven. What do you think they would have talked about?

ACTION TIME:

What country in the world would you like to visit? Can you find it on a map? Can you find out how the message about Jesus first came there? Maybe ask mum and dad, or someone in your church, to help you.

PRAYER TIME:

Dear Lord Jesus, I like to think about you going back to heaven with all the angels cheering you. Thank you that you have promised that one day all your disciples will be able to join in. And thank you for sending Christians all over the world to tell others about you.
Lord, help me to tell others about you. Be with me always. Amen.

27. WHAT WILL JESUS DO IN THE FUTURE?

Jesus had told his disciples again and again that he would leave them. But it must have been a tremendous shock to the disciples when Jesus did finally leave them. A bright cloud came down, and Jesus disappeared.

Peter, James and John had seen that cloud before. Perhaps they thought that when it moved away they would see Jesus again. That was what had happened before on the mountain top. But this time – there was nobody there.

The disciples stood there, looking up into the sky. They couldn't think of anything to say. Two men suddenly appeared, dressed in white. They were God's messengers.

'Why are you standing looking up into the sky?' they asked. 'Jesus is going to come back one day. He'll do it in the same way he went.' The disciples remembered that Jesus had already told them that he was going to come back.

Sometimes people say: 'We don't know what's going to happen in the future.' But we do know one thing that is going to happen. One day – although nobody knows when – Jesus is going to return. But what will he do?

When Jesus returns everyone will see his great power and glory. He will be the Great King. Everyone will bow before him. That will be an absolutely fantastic day.

When Jesus returns, he will raise the bodies of all the people who have died. The people who have trusted in Jesus will get their bodies back – but changed. They will be new and clean and strong – not weak. They will have the kind of body that doesn't get sick and doesn't get tired.

And Jesus will do something else. He will make the whole world new.

Sometimes it seems as if this world is falling to pieces. All kinds of bad things happen in it. It seems out of control. The animals as well as the humans seem to be fighting and killing each other all of the time. Jesus will change all that. The animals and the humans and the whole world will all become friends again.

But there is a sad part. There are people who don't trust and love Jesus. They don't want Jesus to come back. They don't want to serve Jesus now and they don't care about being with Jesus in the future. The sad part is this: they will get what they want. They will be sent away from the presence of Jesus. That will be like going into a place that is totally dark, like night time out in the country with no stars, moon or any light at all.

But when Jesus has made everything new and wonderful, he will do something special. He will take us all to his Father: the people who love him, the animals who serve him, the whole world that he has made new. And he will say: 'Father, we all love you. Here we are. We want to be with you for ever.' And Jesus will lead us to live in God's presence for ever. Fantastic!

27

Question

What will Jesus do in the future?

Answer

Jesus has promised to come back, to make everything new, and to share his kingdom with us for ever and ever.

Jesus has gone back to heaven and is in the presence of his Father. But he hasn't forgotten us. He has promised to come back. Then he will sort everything out that has gone wrong. He will change everything to the way it should be.

When sin came into the world at the beginning, it ruined everything. Even the world we live in has got all kinds of things wrong with it as a result. It doesn't work the way it should. And you just need to watch the animals to see that they can be angry and fight against each other. We do that too.

Jesus is very patient. He has the power to destroy the world. But he doesn't, because he loves it. He wants us to have time to turn away from our sin and to trust in him.
But one day Jesus will return. Then it will be THE END.
But it will also be THE BEGINNING!
He will make everything the way it should be.

Memory Verse

Jesus said: 'I will come back and take you to be with me where I am.'
John chapter 14, verse 3.

ACTIVITIES

READING TIME

You can read about how Jesus will return and what will happen in 1 Corinthians chapter 15, verses 50-58.

TALKING TIME:

Make sure you have had a good listen to the Reading Time passage. Now close your eyes, and try to imagine what will happen. Take turns at describing what you can see!

ACTION TIME:

In the Book of Revelation chapter 22, verses 1-2 there is a wonderful description of part of God's new creation. Can you draw it with coloured pencils, or paint it?

PRAYER TIME:

Dear Lord Jesus, I have never seen you. I don't really know what you look like. But I have learned so much about you from the Bible. I have come to know you and to love you.
Thank you for promising to come back. I can hardly take in that one day I will see you. I'm looking forward to that. It will be wonderful.
Please keep me loving and serving you until then.
Amen

JESUS CALLS US
TO BE HIS DISCIPLES

Questions
28 to 34

28. HOW DOES JESUS TEACH US TO BE HAPPY?

 One day Jesus gathered all his disciples around him. He had already told them about his kingdom. He was to be The Great King. Now he was going to teach them some very important things about how to live in his kingdom. Jesus sat down and began to teach.

'First of all' said Jesus, 'I want to tell you about the happiness God wants you all to have. It is different from what most people think. So listen carefully.' Here's what Jesus went on to say.

Most people think that the best way to become happy is to get plenty of money. But there are very rich people who are very sad. Jesus' way to be happy is to know that you are poor inside because of your sins. Only he can give you what you really need.

Most people think that the way to be happy is to avoid anything that makes you feel sad. Jesus' way is different. You can be happy only when you first become sad! If you are sad about your sinful heart and ask for forgiveness, God will forgive all your sins for Jesus' sake. Then you can be really happy.

Most people think that the way to be happy is to be strong and always to be first. Jesus says the way to be truly happy is different. The only happiness that lasts is letting Jesus do whatever he wants with your life.

Most people think that the way to be happy is by having everything you could ever want. Jesus says that the way to be happy is by asking God to put right all the wrong things in your life.

Most people think that the way to be happy is to look after yourself first. 'Look out for Number One' they say. Jesus says that we can be really happy only when we care for people who are poor and needy and people who have nobody else to help them.

Most people think that the way to be happy is by getting what you want. The glossy magazines have all kinds of adverts telling you about all these things: big cars, marvellous houses, fantastic furniture, looking beautiful. Jesus says you can have all these things and still not be happy. The only thing that can make you happy is having a heart full of love for Jesus himself.

Most people think that the way to be happy is by making sure nobody gets in your way. Jesus says that happiness comes to people who want others to know God's peace.

Most people think they could never be happy if they became disciples of Jesus. They think that if people said or did bad things to you because you belonged to Jesus you would be sad. Jesus says that he has a special happiness to give to his disciples whenever they are alone or in trouble for his sake.

28

Question
How does Jesus teach us to be happy?

Answer
Jesus shows us that being his disciples brings us true happiness. His happiness is real, and it lasts for ever.

Everybody wants to be happy. But lots of people don't know how to be happy. We can be happy only when our lives are working the way God wants them to work. Otherwise things go wrong.

Lots of people think that you can't be a Christian and a happy person. They are sometimes afraid of the cost of following Jesus. What will other people say about me? Will other people call me names? Will they hurt me because I belong to Jesus?

Jesus says that he has a very special happiness to give to us. It is true happiness, and it lasts.

He taught us the way to happiness in his famous Sermon on the Mount. You can find it in Matthew's gospel, chapters 5, 6 and 7. It begins with what grown-ups call The Beatitudes. (A beatitude is one of Jesus' sayings about how to be truly happy).

Memory Verse
Jesus said, 'What good will it be for a man if he gains the whole world, yet forfeits his soul?'
Matthew chapter 16, verse 26.

ACTIVITIES

READING TIME

You will find the Beatitudes in Matthew chapter 5, verses 1-12.

TALKING TIME:
What kind of things do people think will make them happy? Why is it that only Jesus can make us really happy?

ACTION TIME:
Get eight pieces of paper. Put one of your shoes down on the pages and trace a footprint. In each of the footprints write down one of the Beatitudes. Then stick them all together. Put a banner across the top with the words: JESUS MAKES US HAPPY!

PRAYER TIME:
Lord Jesus, thank you for wanting me to be happy. And thank you for giving me so much teaching about happiness. You know that when things go wrong I sometimes doubt your love and care. Help me to be happy because I love you. When I find it hard to be your disciple, please be with me. Thank you for your love for me.
Amen.

29. WHAT DOES JESUS SAY ABOUT BEING REALLY GOOD?

Who likes being good? It isn't easy. In fact, people who think it is easy to be good are in for a surprise! Jesus teaches us that he wants all of his disciples to be really good. Not 'goody-goody', but deep down, all through, all the time good!

Years before Jesus was born a group of people really wanted to live for God and do what he said. They were called Pharisees. They read God's Word and saw what he had commanded in his Law. The Pharisees wanted to keep every command God had given. They knew that wasn't going to be easy. In fact because they knew that we have sinful hearts they saw just how hard it was.

What could they do to help each other keep God's commands? They made up some other commands that would help them to keep the ones God had given them. That might have been quite a good idea. If mum tells you to get up at eight o'clock in the morning, it's a good idea to set your alarm clock at five minutes to eight.   If you're up at five minutes to eight, you'll already be up at eight!

But what do you think of this?

God had told his people to keep one day of the week special. It was called the Sabbath Day (sabbath means rest in Hebrew). They were not to work on that day. To make sure that they didn't do any work, the Pharisees decided what things were work and what things weren't. They added laws of their own to God's laws.

One day Jesus and the disciples were having a walk through the fields on the Sabbath. The disciples had taken some ears of corn from the edges of the field (that was allowed!). They were eating it. Suddenly, out of the corn jumped some Pharisees. 'Aha!' they said (with glee), 'Caught you! You're working on the Sabbath. You have been out here reaping the corn. That's work.' And so they came to Jesus and blamed him. 'Why do your disciples do what is forbidden on the Sabbath?' They were trying to say that Jesus was encouraging people to break the law.

Do you see what had happened? They were far more interested in keeping their own rules than they were in the reasons God had given his rules. What God really meant by his command about the Sabbath day was this. He wanted us to have one day each week when we didn't NEED to work. On that day we can worship him and be with our families. We can rest. We can enjoy being with those who love him.

But these Pharisees were far more interested in keeping the extra rules. They weren't really being good at all. Not deep down, inside, full of love for Jesus goodness.

You can try to keep the rules on your own. But you can't have deep-down goodness without having Jesus' love in your heart. That's what the Pharisees didn't have. But everyone who knows and trusts and loves Jesus has the power of his Spirit to help them to be deep down good!

29

Question

What does Jesus say about being really good?

Answer

Jesus wants his disciples and friends to be really good, with deep down inside goodness. We need his presence and power to be what he wants. That is why Jesus has promised to give each of his followers the help and power of his Holy Spirit.

You don't become really good just by keeping the rules. You could keep the rules outside but in your heart you could still hate them. You can go to church, and even sing the songs — but not really mean them. You can say words in your prayers, but in your heart not really want God to answer them.

So, being good is more difficult than most people think!

The wonderful good news Jesus brings is this. First he died on the cross so that our sins can be forgiven. But, second, Jesus gives us his own Spirit so that we can have his own goodness deep down in our hearts. When we have Jesus' goodness in our hearts, we begin to want to be really good, deep down good!

Memory Verse:

Jesus said: 'Unless your righteousness (goodness) surpasses (is better than) that of the Pharisees and the teachers of the law, you will certainly not enter the kingdom of heaven.'

Matthew chapter 5, verse 20.

ACTIVITIES

Jesus' teaching on being really good can be found in Matthew chapter 5, verses 21-48.

TALKING TIME:

Do you find it hard to be good? What do you find hard about it? In what ways do you think Jesus can help you?

ACTION TIME:

Paul calls being really good 'the fruit of the Spirit' in his letter to the Galatians, chapter 5, verses 22 and 23.
Can you make a paper tree with big branches and nine different kinds of fruits on it? Write the name of one of the fruits of the Spirit mentioned by Paul on each piece of fruit.

PRAYER TIME:

Lord Jesus, thank you that you are good. You are really and truly, deep down, always good.
You know that sometimes I don't even want to be good. And sometimes when I want to be

good I do bad things. Please forgive me. Please fill my heart with your love so that I can become deep down and really good.
Thank you, Lord Jesus for being such a loving and patient friend to me. Amen.

30. HOW CAN JESUS HELP ME TO BE TRUE?

Remember the Pharisees? They were the ones Jesus spoke about who looked a lot better on the outside than they did on the inside. But were they really good, even on the outside?

People who love God want to serve God. They want to give to those who are in need. They want to pray for God to work in the world. They want to say 'no' to themselves so that they can see and do what pleases God most of all.

The Pharisees did all of these things. They gave to the poor; they prayed; on two days of the week they didn't eat food to show that they could say 'no' to themselves. You would think they must have been deep down good. It looked on the outside as though they were. But Jesus saw that they were really living a lie. In fact, Jesus said, 'Look a little closer on the outside. You'll be shocked by what you see.'

There is a special word used in the New Testament for them: hypocrite. It means somebody who pretends to be different from what he or she really is.

When the hypocrites gave to the poor, they made sure that people were looking. They wanted everyone to see how much they gave. Instead of caring about the poor, they were only wanting people to see them and praise them. They were really buying people's praises.

When the hypocrites prayed, they made a great big show of it. They would stand at the corner of the street to do it. Everyone could see them. People said 'Look, that man must be a wonderful man; he is praying to God.' But they were really only asking people to praise them.

Imagine not eating your dinner because you wanted to spend more time thinking about God and praying to him. Could you do that two days every week? You would think anyone who did that must really love the Lord. But when the hypocrites went without food, they made sure everyone knew it. They rubbed stuff on their faces to make themselves look hungry and weak. They were just actors. Maybe they didn't even go without the food. But people saw them and said 'Look at him! He looks ill. He must have been doing without food and spending time with God.'

All the time the hypocrites looked as though their hearts were full of love to God. But in fact they were looking out of the corner of their eyes to see if people were watching them. They were trying to hear if people were praising them. It was all an act.

If we really love God, Jesus said, we'll not care what other people think. We'll be happy to give to needy people without anyone knowing. We'll pray where only God can see us. When we say 'no' to something we like so we can be with God, we'll have a smile on our face.

30

Question

How can Jesus help me to be true?

Answer

Jesus wants us to love and serve him with all our hearts. He doesn't like us to pretend. He wants us to be real. Remember that Jesus is always watching us. Remember that Jesus is worth doing everything for.

Jesus doesn't want us to be pretend disciples.
Sometimes people pretend to be better than they really are. And sometimes they do that so that we will think they are better than they really are. Jesus had a special word to describe that: hypocrisy.

A hypocrite is really an actor. Hypocrites pretend to be different people from who they really are. But there's no point in pretending to Jesus. He can see behind the mask. He knows what we are really like.

Because Jesus loves us, we don't need to pretend when we're in his presence. He will always forgive us when we sin and ask for forgiveness. He will always help us when we tell him we need him.

Memory Verse

Jesus said: 'Your Father, who sees what is done in secret, will reward you.'
        Matthew chapter 6, verse 4.

ACTIVITIES

READING TIME

Read on in The Sermon on the Mount to discover what Jesus had to say about hypocrites. You will find his teaching in Matthew chapter 6, verses 1-18.

TALKING TIME:

Do you think that Christians today sometimes pretend to be better than they really are? How can we be real and true, just as Jesus wants us to be?

ACTION TIME:

Can you draw three cartoon pictures of the different things Jesus said the hypocrites do?

PRAYER TIME:

Lord Jesus, you know I want other people to like me. I want other people to say good and nice things about me. I know that's not wrong. But I want what YOU think of me to be the most important thing. Please help me always to remember that you are with me. Help me to remember that you are watching and that you can see me. Help me to do everything for you first.

Thank you for your great love for me. Thank you for dying so that even hypocrites could be forgiven and changed. Thank you that you are always with me. Amen.

31. HOW DOES JESUS TEACH ME TO PRAY?

One of the things that amazed Jesus' disciples was this: Jesus loved to pray.

Jesus told the disciples that when some people pray they aren't really talking to God about the needs of others. He said that they're really just talking to the people who are watching them. All they're interested in is people praising them for being holy.

Jesus was different. When he prayed he was really talking to God as his Father. Sometimes he prayed with his disciples. They could tell that he prayed in a different way from them. He really knew and loved God. He spoke to God as his Father. It was amazing to hear him pray.

The Lord Jesus wants his disciples to be able to pray the way he did. So, in his famous Sermon on the Mount, he taught them about how they could speak to the Heavenly Father. He gave them a kind of outline prayer, to help them see the things they should talk to God about.

When we pray to God as our Father, we can tell him that we know he is good. That is just like telling him that we love him very much.

What should we ask for, first of all? Do you remember that Jesus taught that God's kingdom had come near? Well, we can pray that God's kingdom – his reign – will be seen all over the world. God's will is always done in heaven. We can pray that it will be done on earth too. That's saying that we want to do our Father's will. Is that what you want?

The Father cares about us. He knows that we need his help very much indeed. How can we ask him for what we really need?

The wonderful thing about the way Jesus teaches us to pray is that he knows exactly what we really need. We think we need lots and lots of things. But Jesus says we only need a few things. Here they are:

First we need food and clothes and things like that. That's why Jesus says we should ask God to give us what we need each day.

Second, we need to remember that we have sinned. In fact we are like people who can't pay what we owe. We call that being a debtor. There is no way we can repay the debt we owe to God. Jesus says: 'Ask God to cancel the debts of your sins!'

Third, Jesus teaches us to remember that we are weak. We don't have the power we need to be able to fight against temptation. We certainly can't overcome the Devil in our own strength. So we need to ask our Father to protect us.

Whenever you pray, remember the outline prayer Jesus taught his disciples. It will help you talk to your Father in heaven about everything.

31

Question

How does Jesus teach me to pray?

Answer

Jesus wants us to be able to tell our Father everything about ourselves. And he wants us to know that our Heavenly Father is so great and good that he listens to our prayers. That is why Jesus taught his disciples what we call The Lord's Prayer.

Sometimes it seems quite easy to pray. But at other times we feel sleepy and lazy, or we can't think what to say. Sometimes, if we're honest about it, we don't want to pray.

Jesus – as always – can help us.

Do you know how to do jig-saw puzzles? First of all you put together the pieces that go round the edge. Then it is much easier to fill it in.

Jesus has given us an outline prayer. We can fill it in with our own prayers.

If you ever find it hard to pray, remember the outline Jesus has given you. Begin with one of the things he tells us to pray about. Think about what that means. Then you will begin to speak to the Heavenly Father about other things too.

Memory Verse

Jesus said: 'When you pray, do not keep on babbling like pagans, for they think they will be heard because of their many words. Do not be like them, for your Father knows what you need before you ask him.'

Matthew chapter 6, verses 7 and 8

ACTIVITIES

READING TIME

The prayer Jesus taught his disciples is in Matthew chapter 6, verses 9-13.

TALKING TIME:

What kinds of things can you pray for today? For yourself? For your family? For your friends?

ACTION TIME:

Draw some big boxes. Inside each of them write one of the things that Jesus tells us to pray about.

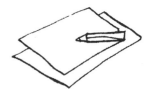

Then add, inside the box, some other things like them that you want to speak to the Heavenly Father about.

PRAYER TIME:

Our Father in heaven,
hallowed be your name,
your kingdom come,
your will be done
on earth as it is in heaven.
Give us today our daily bread.
Forgive us our debts,
as we also have forgiven our debtors.
And lead us not into temptation,
but deliver us from the evil one.
Amen.

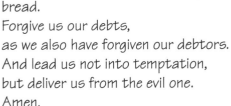

32. WHAT KINDS OF THINGS CAN SPOIL MY LOVE FOR JESUS?

When Jesus began to tell people about the kingdom of God they got very excited. Crowds came to hear Jesus teach and to see the great things he did. They loved to listen to Jesus. They loved what he did.

Then Jesus began to explain what it means to be one of his disciples. It seemed very difficult.

The people wanted Jesus to show them his power. They wanted Jesus to do something about their diseases. But they didn't want Jesus to do anything about their sin. And they certainly didn't want Jesus to ask them to give up everything to be his disciples.So the crowds began to drift away.

Soon Jesus was left with the disciples who really loved him and wanted to be faithful to him. Even they ran away when Jesus was arrested. They were scared. But they did really love him, and he knew that. Some of them came back to be with him when he was dying. And, of course, he loved them and came back to them first when he rose again.

It is the same for us today. Jesus calls us to follow him. But there are many things that can get in the way. We can begin to love other things first and Jesus only second. Then it will not be long before love for Jesus is in third place, and then in fourth place . . . and soon we will not love him at all.

This does not happen to Jesus' real disciples. One way we know we are really his disciples is by making sure nothing gets in the way of our love for him. Jesus told his disciples that there are two things that can easily get in the way and spoil our love for him.

One thing that can spoil our love for Jesus is setting our hearts on things that we want to get. We see lots of things it would be nice to have. Then we feel we want to have them. And then we feel we need them; we can't do without them. Then these things have become idols. We are worshipping them. And we stop loving Jesus.

Another thing that can spoil our love is worrying about things. Sometimes we worry about our appearance. We think:'What do other people think of me? Do they like the way I look?' Lots of magazines today tell you to worry about these things, don't they?

But Jesus says we don't need to worry about these things. After all, God feeds and clothes the birds and the flowers. And you are much, much more important to God than either a bird or a flower.

What Jesus says isn't hard to understand. And it's all true. He doesn't ask us to do great big complicated things. He asks us to trust his Father. And we know we can trust him, because we know his Son – Jesus.

32

Question

What kinds of things can spoil my love for Jesus?

Answer

Sometimes people who once said they wanted to be disciples begin to love other things instead of Jesus. They love getting and having more than they love him.

Jesus once said that we set our hearts on whatever we think is most important. If loving him is the most important thing in our lives we will not let anything spoil that love.

Does loving Jesus first mean that we lose everything else? Lots of people think that it does. But Jesus promises that our Heavenly Father will give us everything that we need.

One day Simon Peter asked Jesus if becoming a disciple meant that you just lose everything and get nothing in return. 'Not at all' Jesus told him. In fact Jesus promised Peter that he would get back a hundred times everything Jesus asked him to leave behind in order to follow him. That is a great promise. Always remember it.

MemoryVerse:

Jesus said: 'Where your treasure is, there your heart will be also.'

Matthew chapter 6, verse 21.

ACTIVITIES

READING TIME

Jesus' teaching on things that can spoil our love for him can be found in Matthew chapter 6, verses 19-34.

TALKING TIME:

Do you ever worry? What kinds of things do you worry about? How do Jesus' promises help you not to worry?

ACTION TIME:

Get a piece of paper, and draw a line down the middle of it.

In the left hand column, write down all the things that people like to have.

Then, in the right hand column, write the name 'Jesus.' Underneath Jesus' name write down what he gives to his disciples.

Which column do you think is more valuable?

PRAYER TIME:

Dear Lord Jesus, my love for you doesn't seem to stay the same. Some days I feel I love you a lot. But other days I feel tempted to love things that don't really matter all that much.

Please help me always to love you first. And please help me to feel how much you love me.

Thank you for loving me first, long before I loved you.

Amen.

33. HOW DOES JESUS TEACH ME TO BE WISE?

Jesus wants all of his followers to be wise.

We usually think that to be wise you need to be old. Sometimes we think that wise people all seem to have grey hair and spectacles and are too old to work any more. Some old people really are wise. They have thought about everything that has happened to them. They see how things work best. That's what it means to be wise: to know how to get things to work for the best.

But Jesus can help us to be wise long before we're old.

When Jesus was teaching his disciples in The Sermon on the Mount, he gave them five important lessons about being really wise. Here they are;

Lesson One: Don't talk or act as though you know everything. You will end up trying to put everyone right. And you'll not notice that there are wrong things in your own life. People who are always complaining about others don't see their own faults. When you have dealt with your own faults you will really be able to help others.

Lesson Two: Some people don't see any faults in others. That's not wise either. Jesus said something like this: 'You wouldn't take your mother's pearl necklace and throw it into a pig pen and expect the pig to put it on and look beautiful, would you?' So, if you speak to a friend about Jesus and they don't want to listen, you shouldn't just go on and on at them. Wait for the right time. That's being wise.

Lesson Three: Trust God as your Heavenly Father. He will give you everything you really need. Good fathers give their children what they need, don't they? So why not trust the Great and Good Father? And if you are in his family, one of the things you will do is this. You will think: What would I like others to do for me? If you know the answer, then you should do the same for them.

Lesson Four: It isn't easy to be a disciple of Jesus. It is like going through a narrow door and walking along a narrow road – when everyone else has crowded through a broad door and is walking on a broad road. So, you need to make a decision. And you need to know that Jesus' way is not the easier way. But there's something else you need to know. The narrow road is the only one that leads to life with Jesus.

Lesson Five: There are some people who pretend to be followers of Jesus. But they are really only interested in themselves. They want others to do what they say. They sometimes become leaders. These false disciples can sound very true. They will tell you 'We have the truth.' How can you tell the difference between a person who is a true disciple and leader and one who is false? Watch out for the way they live. Do they love Jesus? Are they humble, like Jesus? Does their teaching help you to love and serve Jesus? Or are they really more interested in themselves?

These lessons will help you to be wise.

33

Question

How does Jesus teach me to be wise?

Answer

Jesus helps me to be wise by showing me how his teaching works in my life. He teaches me how to please him and to live for him in a sinful world.

The Bible is full of wisdom. Wisdom is being able to work things out in the best possible way. God is wise—he does everything in the best possible way.

One of the Psalms in the Old Testament tells us that God's teaching can make us even wiser than the old people. It can even make us wiser than our teachers.

Jesus was wise. He was very, very wise. He had thought a lot about God's Word. He loved to see how he could put it into practice. God's Word told Jesus what was really in people's hearts. So he knew how to speak to them.

How do we become wise? We become wise the same way Jesus did. We read the Bible. We think about what it says. We ask him to help us to do what it says.

Wisdom isn't something you can get in a day. It takes time. But it's worth its weight in gold!

MemoryVerse

From infancy you have known the holy Scriptures which are able to make you wise for salvation through faith in Christ Jesus.

2 Timothy chapter 3, verse 15.

ACTIVITIES

READING TIME

Jesus' teaching on how to live wisely is in Matthew chapter 7, verses 1-23.

TALKING TIME:

Can you think of different times when you need to have wisdom to know what to do? How could you put into practice the lessons Jesus teaches?

ACTION TIME:

Read Lesson 4 again and draw a route map to heaven. Remember that the gate, road and any bridges should all be narrow. Underneath your map write out these verses: John chapter 14, verse 6 and Matthew chapter 7, verse 14.

PRAYER TIME:

Lord Jesus, you are very wise. But I am sometimes foolish. I do the wrong things. I say the wrong things. I need your help. Please teach me how to be wise. And please help me to be patient so that I will learn all the lessons you teach me.

Thank you, Lord Jesus, that you know best. Thank you that you want me always to choose the best.

Amen.

34. HOW CAN I GIVE MY LIFE FOR JESUS?

This is the end of *The Big Book of Questions and Answers about Jesus*. We have learned a lot about him, haven't we? – from the time of his birth right through to the time of his coming back again. We have learned about what Jesus said. We have learned about what Jesus did. And we have just been learning about how Jesus teaches us to live for him. It is time to ask a question:

Are you one of Jesus' disciples? Can you answer 'Yes'?

At the end of his Sermon on the Mount, Jesus speaks about what it means to be one of his disciples. Here is what Jesus said:

Living is a bit like putting up a house. Imagine two neighbours decided to build new houses at the same time. One just started building his house on the ground. Soon he was up to the top floor, the roof was on, and he was living in his new home.

But the other man took a lot longer. He didn't start by building up. He built *down* ! He started digging and digging down into the ground until he hit rock. Then, on top of the rock, he started building upwards. Eventually the second man's house was built. Although it took him a lot longer his house looked more or less the same as the other man's. The first man must have thought he'd been a lot smarter.

Some time later there was a great storm. Both men looked out of their windows to see what was happening. The sky was dark, and the rain was pouring down. This went on day after day. The town river began to flood. Soon the water was running down the street. At the same time there were gale force winds. It was awful. The man who had built his house just on the ground had made a big mistake. The water got into the soil, and the house began to slide. Suddenly there was a tremendous crash – and the house fell to pieces!

When he heard the noise of the crash outside, the other man rushed to his bedroom window to see what had happened. He looked at where his neighbour's house had been. It was gone! But his own house was safe. He had built it on a solid foundation of rock. His house could survive the terrible storm. The man thought to himself, 'Why did my neighbour not listen to me? I told him he needed to build his house on a good, solid foundation.'

'Are you going to be like the foolish man who built on sand, or like the wise man who built on the solid rock?' Jesus asked.

What did Jesus mean? He meant that our lives are like buildings. If we don't have a strong foundation, we will not be able to last as Jesus' disciples.

Jesus himself is the Rock on which we can build our lives. He wants us to turn away from our sins, to trust in him, to love him and to live for him. If you do that, no matter what storms may come, you will be able to stand for ever.

34

Question

How can I give my life for Jesus?

Answer

When Jesus calls us to be his disciples he wants us to do two things.

He calls us to trust in him as our Saviour and to follow him as our Lord. Jesus promises that he will care for us and help us all through life. Then he will take us to be with him forever.

Knowing and loving Jesus is the biggest and most important thing in life. When we come to Jesus and ask him to be our Saviour, he forgives all of our sins. He brings us into his kingdom and makes us his disciples.

To follow Jesus means that we turn away from our sins. We hold his hand tight, and he holds ours in his. He guards us all the time. Even when things seem to go wrong, he is still holding on to us.

When we feel things are too difficult, Jesus will stay beside us. Jesus will never leave us.

Trusting and following Jesus is like building a house on a deep, strong foundation. It can never be knocked down.

So, before you come to the end of *The Big Book of Questions and Answers about Jesus*, make sure that you have begun to trust him. Make sure you are his disciple.

MemoryVerse

Jesus said: 'I am the light of the world. Whoever follows me will never walk in darkness, but will have the light of life.'
John chapter 8, verse 12.

ACTIVITIES

READING TIME

Jesus' story of the two men who built houses can be found in Matthew chapter 7, verses 24-28.

TALKING TIME:

Jesus says that people can build their lives on foundations that won't last. What kinds of things do you think he had in mind? What is the only foundation that really will last?

ACTION TIME:

Can you find out what houses would have looked like when Jesus was alive? Then draw four pictures which show the story Jesus told.

PRAYER TIME:

Lord Jesus, I want to thank you for all that you have taught me about yourself. Thank you that there is so much I can learn about your love. Please help me always to remember that you are my Rock. You will keep me.
Lord, I am weak, but you are very, very strong.
Please keep me following you.
Please help me to trust you. And please help me to love you forever.
Amen.

INDEX OF QUESTIONS

QUESTION   **PAGE**

WHEN JESUS WAS A BOY

WHEN JESUS LEFT HOME

JESUS THE GREAT TEACHER

JESUS THE GREAT SAVIOUR

QUESTION	PAGE

JESUS GOES TO THE CROSS

JESUS CALLS US TO BE HIS DISCIPLES

The Author

Sinclair B Ferguson

Sinclair B Ferguson is senior pastor of First Presbyterian Church, Columbia, South Carolina. He is Distinguished Visiting Professor of Systematic Theology at Westminster Theological Seminary Dallas, Texas.

Sinclair has written extensively on the Christian Faith. His books are written out of conviction that biblical teaching builds strong Christians; a number of his works are available in several languages.

Sinclair and Dorothy Ferguson have four children of their own. Like all parents they know the challenges that face families today. Realising how difficult it can be to find reliable books to help children understand about the Lord Jesus Christ and the Christian Faith, Dr. Ferguson has written *The Big Book of Questions and Answers about Jesus* and *The Big Book of Questions and Answers about the Christian Faith.*

These books are designed to help children and their parents and teachers to:

*   ... understand the Bible.
*   ... to talk about the Bible naturally.
*   ... grow strong in their own faith in a world of tremendous spiritual and moral confusion and uncertainty.

ISBN: 978-1-85792-295-0

**What people said about
Sinclair Ferguson's book:
The Big Book of Questions and Answers
A Family Guide to the Christian Faith**

"A book providing the answers to some of the many questions which children are bound to raise when learning about Christianity. It is an ideal resource for parents to teach their child(ren) about Christianity."

*CY Magazine
Church Pastoral Aid Society*

"It is Biblically sound, with well thought out answers and good suggestions for discussion, follow-up actions and prayers. The format is straight forward and easy to follow. If you have family study times this could be for you."

*Jane Rowe
CLC Book Reviews*

"A book for families to discover the key doctrines of Christianity in a way that stimulates discussion and helps children want to know more."

Covenanter Witness

CBC Children's Book of the Year Winnner

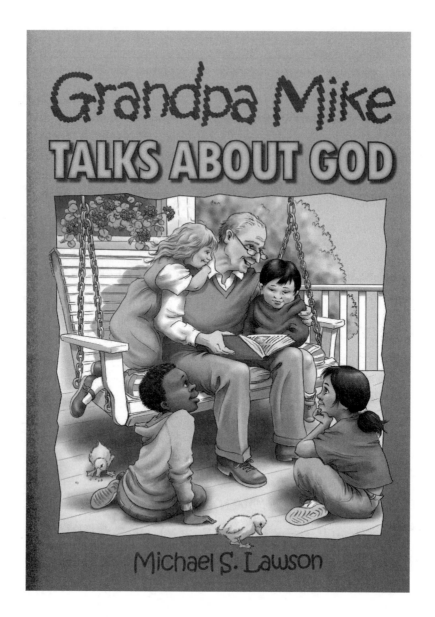

ISBN: 978-1-84550-250-8

Grandpa Mike
TALKS ABOUT GOD

We love it when people sit us down to tell us a story. Hey! Grandpa Mike, tell us a story!

Storytelling is an ideal way of teaching children. So let's find out why we should love God with thirty five stories from Grandpa Mike - each one is based around a special word [see the list below], a word that describes God. They don't tell you everything about God but they do tell you some of the most important things you need to know.

Through these charming and captivating stories, you will find out that God is waiting to meet with you - how about starting right now, says Grandpa Mike!

God is adorable; angry; beautiful; colorful; creative; everywhere; fair; faithful; famous; friend; generous; gentle; holy; huge; invisible; joy; kind; life; light; love; merciful; mysterious; patient; playful; righteous; scary; smart (omniscient); spirit; strong (omnipotent); tender; timeless; a trinity; truth and unique.

"Dr. Lawson, AKA Grandpa Mike, makes the nourishment of theology appealing to kids. What a wonderful and needed contribution to our diets! This volume holds the promise of training our children and grandchildren to put their confidence in God and not forget the works of his hands."
Dr. Michael Easley, President, Moody Bible Institute

"Grandpa Mike's gentle, down-to-earth book encourages children to get to know God in a deeper, fuller way. Aimed straight at the child who is beginning to wonder about his or her faith Lawson opens up theology in an age-appropriate way. Not cotton candy or simplistic, this book is a great one for parents and children to discuss together, and when they have digested it, they will have a better understanding of God than many seminary students."
Marlene LeFever, Vice President of Educational Resources, Cook Communications Ministries

Michael Lawson (a.k.a. Grandpa Mike) is the Department Chair and Senior Professor of Christian Education at Dallas Theological Seminary - and wants it known that he has at least six more hairs on the top of his head than the picture on the cover!

Children's Teaching & Guidance

On The Way for 3-9's

ISBN: 978-1-85792-301-8

We would all like our lesson plans on the Christian faith to be easier to prepare, balanced and effective. Do you also want your lessons to encourage children to view the Bible as a fascinating guide, utterly relevant to their lives? **TnT** have developed *On The Way* to be all that and more...

Edited by David Jackman, *On The Way* has been used in a growing number of churches throughout the world. With the complete series, you will have all you need to give your children from age 3-9 a comprehensive insight to the Bible's teaching.

Benefits of On The Way

* Undated material
* Encourages leaders to study the Bible for themselves
* 3 age related activities
* Chronological approach to teaching the Bible
* Suitable for use in Sunday Schools, Homeschooling or as part of your Christian School syllabus.
* 14 Books in total.
* Three year syllabus

'Biblical ignorance is a plague not only in the land but in the churches. This material will cure the problem by giving the children firm foundations in scriptural knowledge from their earliest years.'
Dick Lucas, St Helens Church, London

ISBN: 978-1-85792-409-1

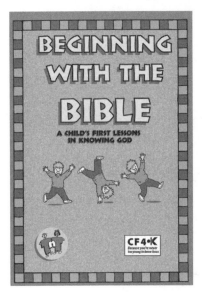

Children can and should be taught from the very earliest age about the God who made them and loves them. *Beginning with the Bible* is a three book series that is designed to help parents and teachers to simply and clearly explain some of the fundemental truths of the Christian message to the very youngest children.

With stories, activities, games and craft ideas for each session, *Beginning with the Bible* gives you three terms of fundamental input for young children. The lessons can be taught at home, in a playgroup or as a 'pre Sunday School' class.

The materials, thoroughly tried and tested by **TnT Ministries**, are intelligible, usable, biblically accurate, and take the job of teaching seriously.
ISBN: 978-1-85792-224-0
ISBN: 978-1-85792-445-9
ISBN: 978-1-85792-454-1

For more information on this series including the new TnT 9-11's series of books please contact Christian Focus Publications for a syllabus.

The Mission Zone

Produced by Mark and Joanne Ellis.
Co-sponsored by Overseas Missionary Fellowship
If you are teaching 7-11 year olds, you need this book.
Let the children taste new cultures and meet colourful characters.

A creative blend of facts, games, crafts and ideas.
User-friendly and flexible. Easy to adapt to fit the needs of your group.
Ideal for dipping into or using week by week.
All you need for a five minute slot or a two-hour session.

ISBN: 978-1-85792-446-6

The Mission Zone

'This get's inside the lives of people from another culture. An essential resource for launching children into the adventure of missions. Prepare for take off!'
Stephen Nichols, All Souls Langham Place

'Full of good ideas to help teach 7-11 year olds the importance of mission. An area that has long been neglected in children's ministry. Every Sunday School should buy a copy.'
Thalia Blundell, TnT Ministries.

'This took the glazed look out of my eyes when thinking about missions. It grabs your attention, it's fun, it's easy to use, and it's full of creative ideas.'
Hazel Scrimshire, Youth worker,
St. Paul's & St. George's, Edinburgh.

'Cor cool!'
Shona Clements, age 11.

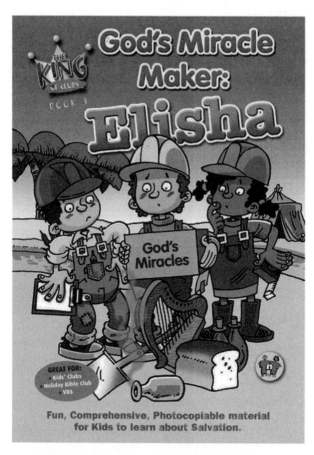

ISBN: 978-1-84550-291-1

God's Miracle Maker: Elisha

The Alternative way of doing a Holiday Bible Club Programme!
'Non-yucky' teaching about salvation through Jesus to your children's club over 6 weeks (or six days for a holiday club/VBS programme!)
Do you want your children to relaise that the Bible is God's relevant, exciting and dynamic guide.
God's miracle worker has superb games, thoughtful activities and a thorough explanation of the gospel message. This material that brings children to focus on fun, faith, and God's forgiveness.
In the amazing world of 'God's Miracle Maker' you wil come accross the case of gruesome poison, the incident of the blind soldiers as well as the multiplying oil.
God's Miracle Maker does not shrink from teaching about sin, judgement and forgiveness as well as God's plan of redemption!

Reviews

"Very good... ideas that look really interesting. I would recommend this series.'"
Simon Hoggarth (age 13), Education Otherwise

"Excellent, enjoyable. It has been tested in many different churches and denominations and comes with the highest recommendation."
Ann MacAskill, The Monthly Record

"This is a comprehensive scheme for children to be introduced to Bible stories. Recommended."
Sarah Cook, Association of Christian Teachers

King of Clubs
Other titles in the King of Clubs series:

God's Zoo   ISBN: 978-1-84559-069-6

God's Secret Agent - Joseph   ISBN: 978-1-84550-113-6

CHRISTIAN FOCUS PUBLICATIONS

Christian Focus / Christian Heritage / CF4K / Mentor

Christian Focus Publications publishes books for adults and children under its four main imprints: Christian Focus, CF4K, Mentor and Christian Heritage. Our books reflect that God's word is reliable and Jesus is the way to know him, and live for ever with him.

Our children's publication list includes a Sunday school curriculum that covers pre-school to early teens; puzzle and activity books. We also publish personal and family devotional titles, biographies and inspirational stories that children will love.

If you are looking for quality Bible teaching for children then we have an excellent range of Bible story and age specific theological books.

From pre-school to teenage fiction, we have it covered!

Find us at our web page: www.christianfocus.com

CF4•K
Because you're never too young to know Jesus